A Walk Through the Mountains

A Bee's Life Press

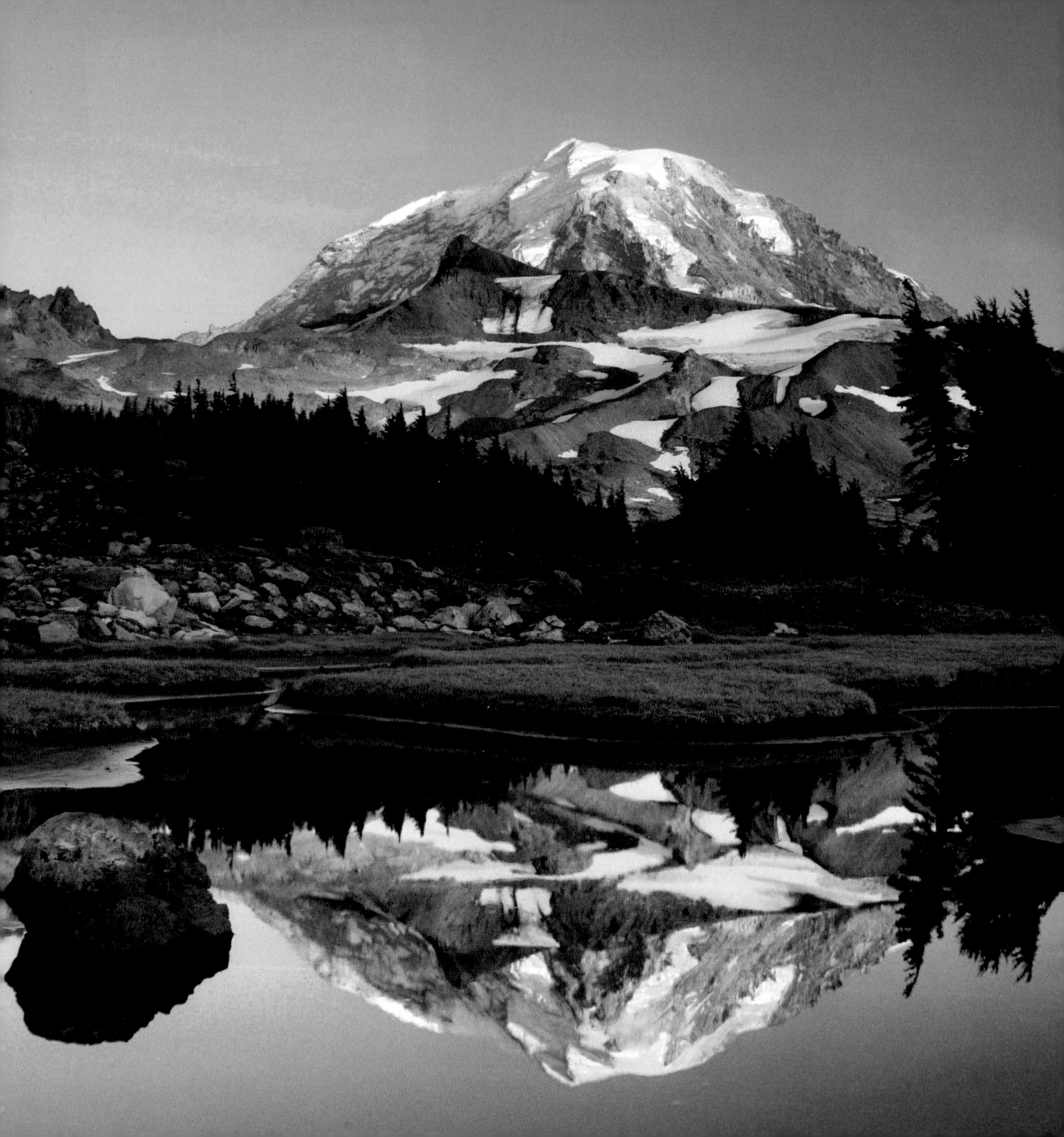

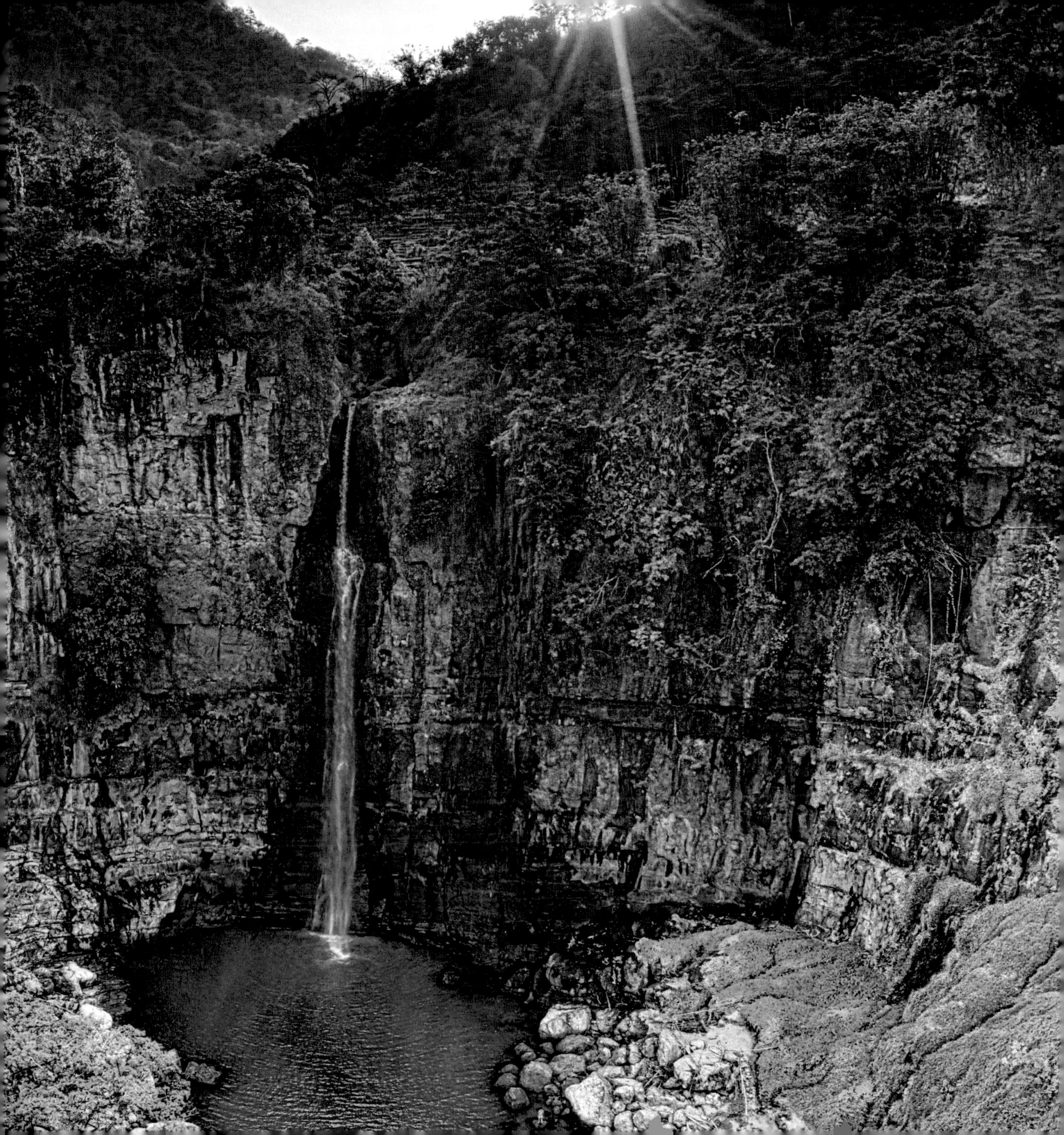

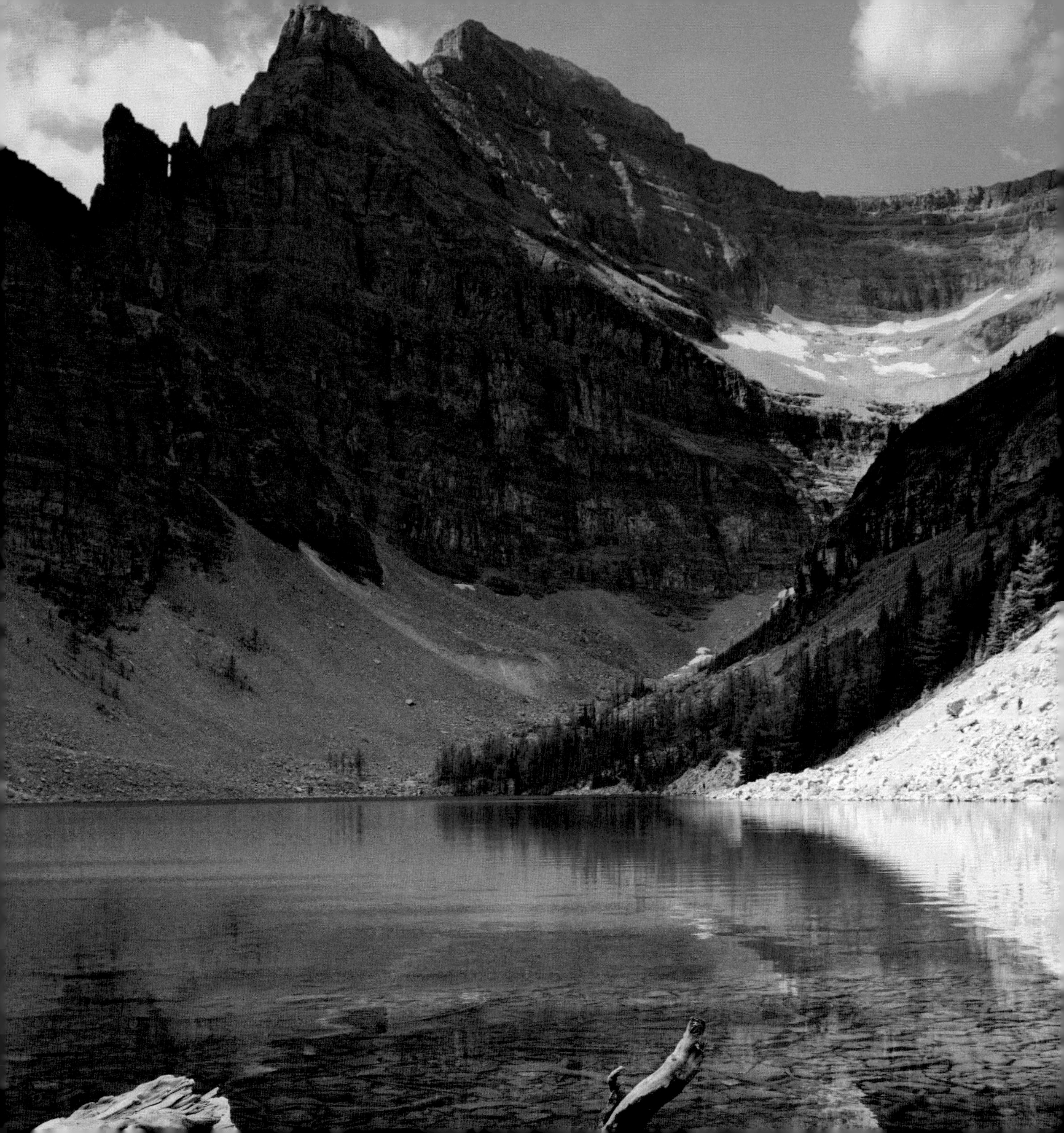

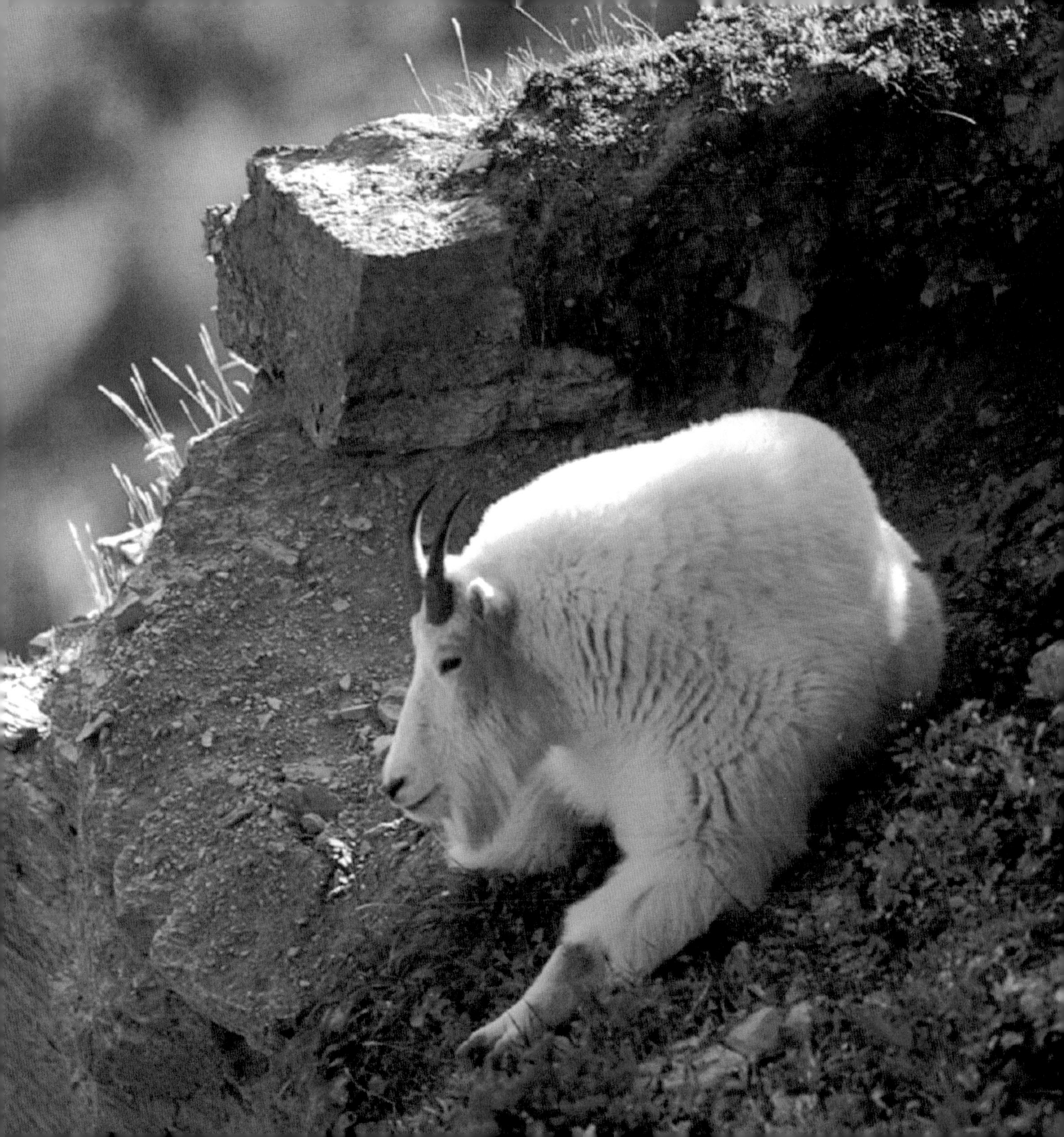

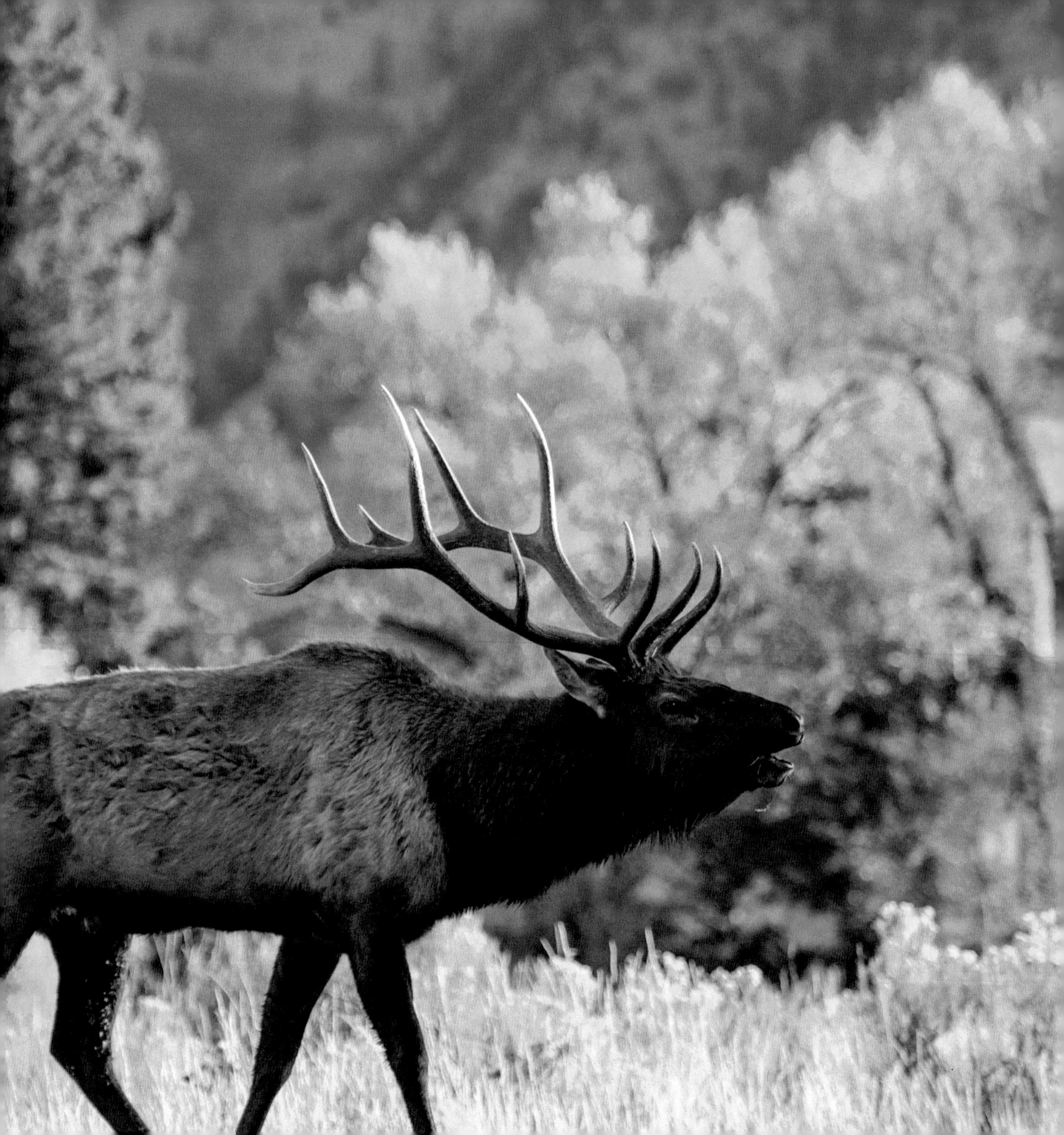

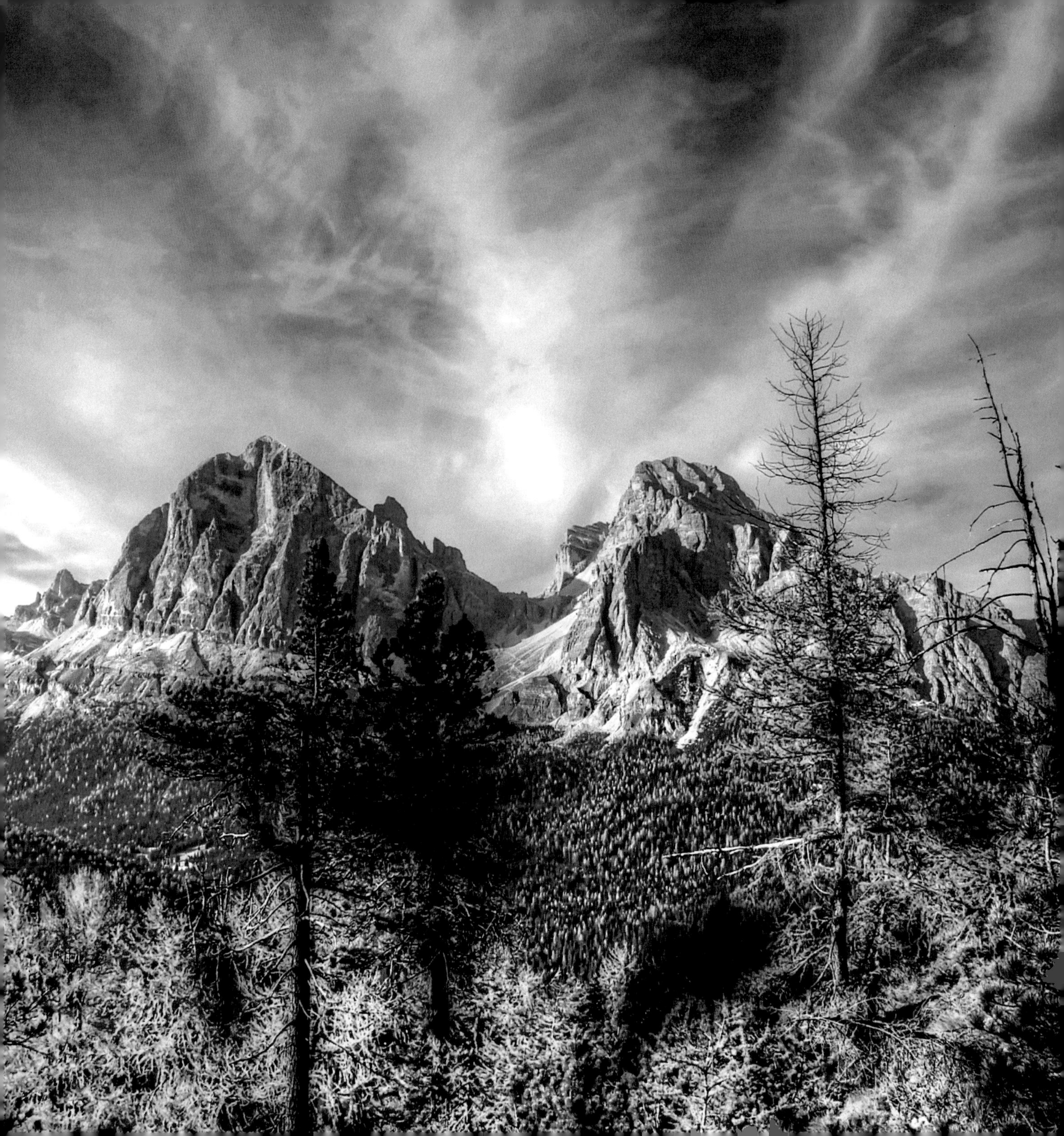

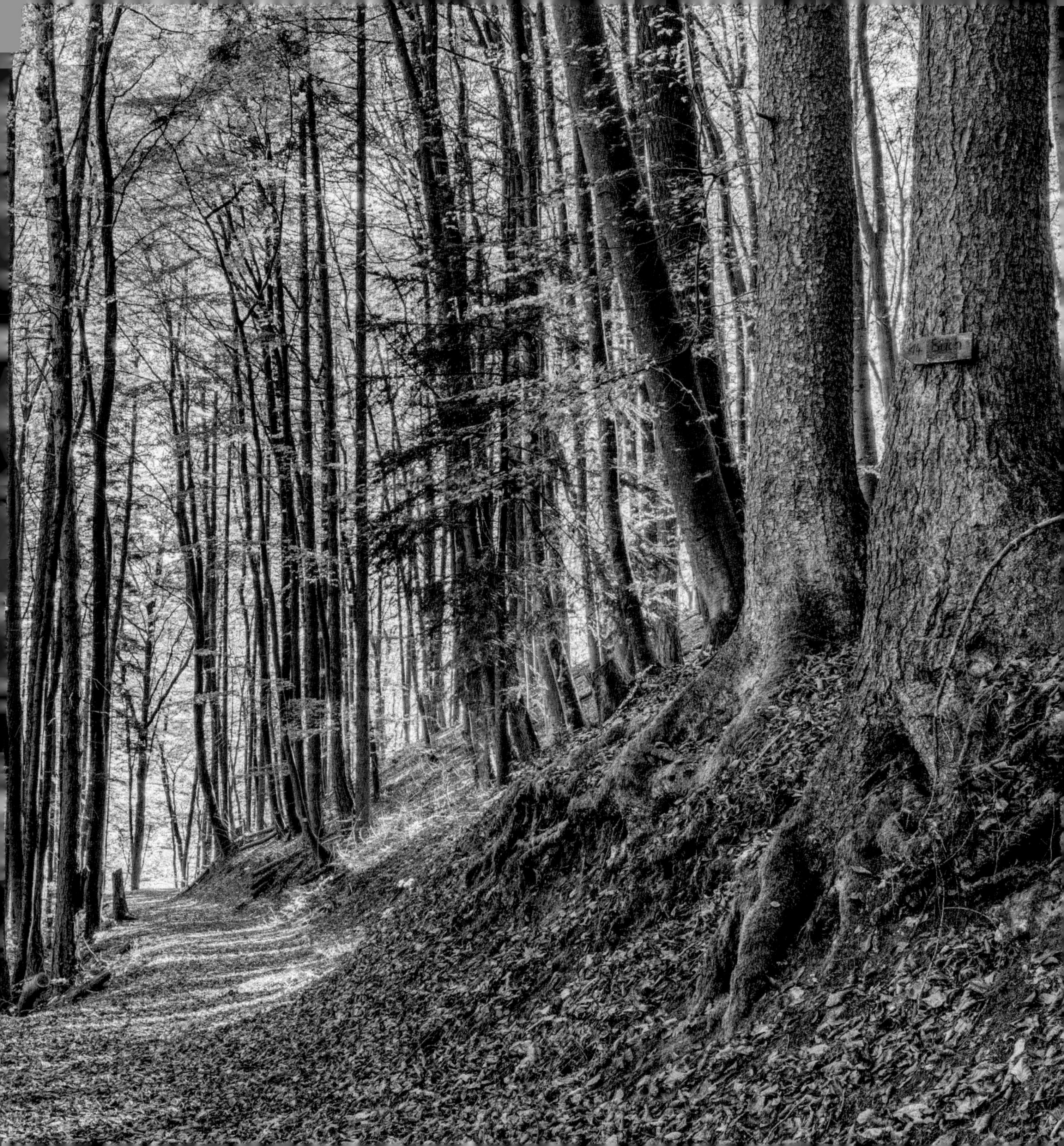

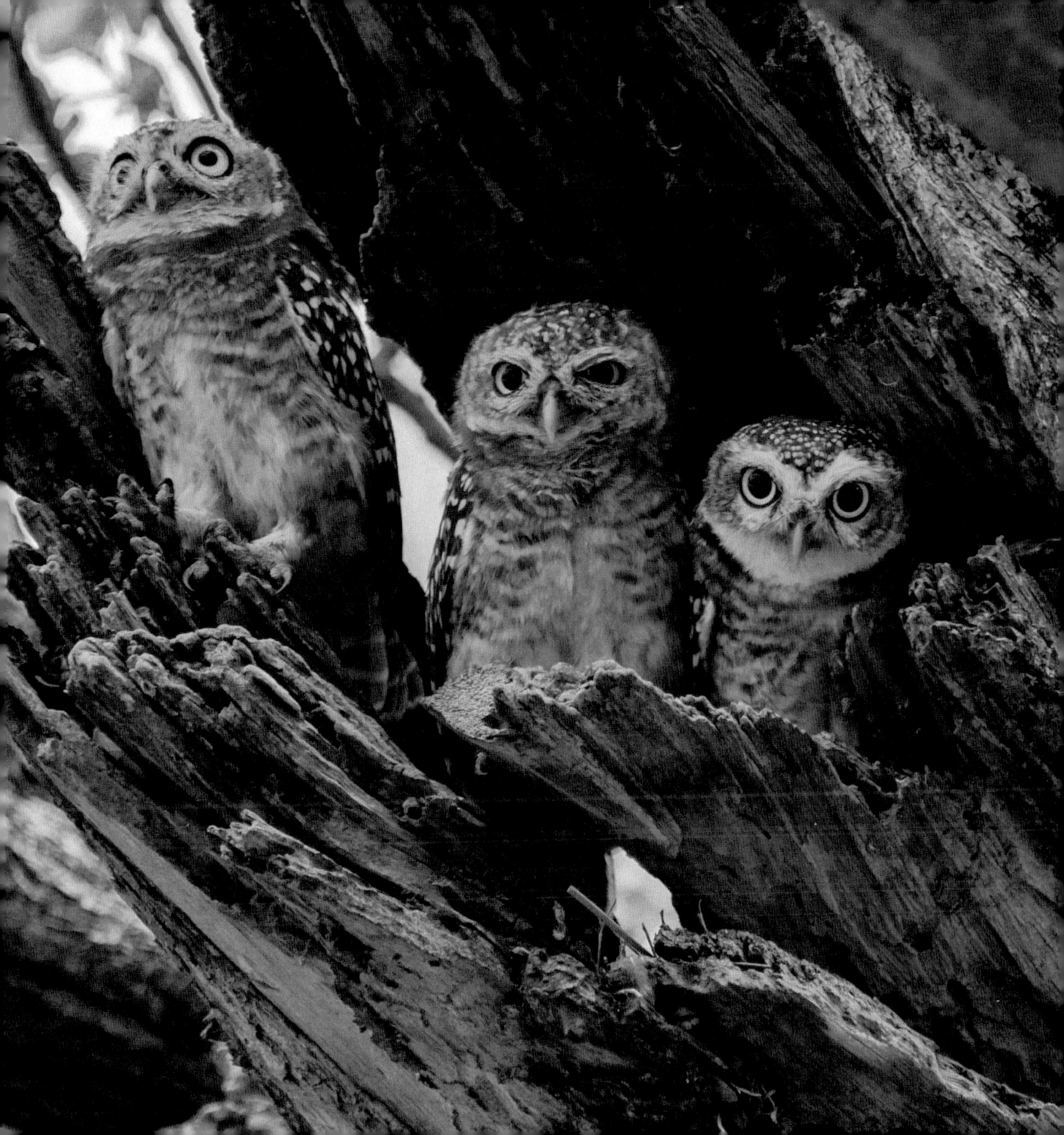

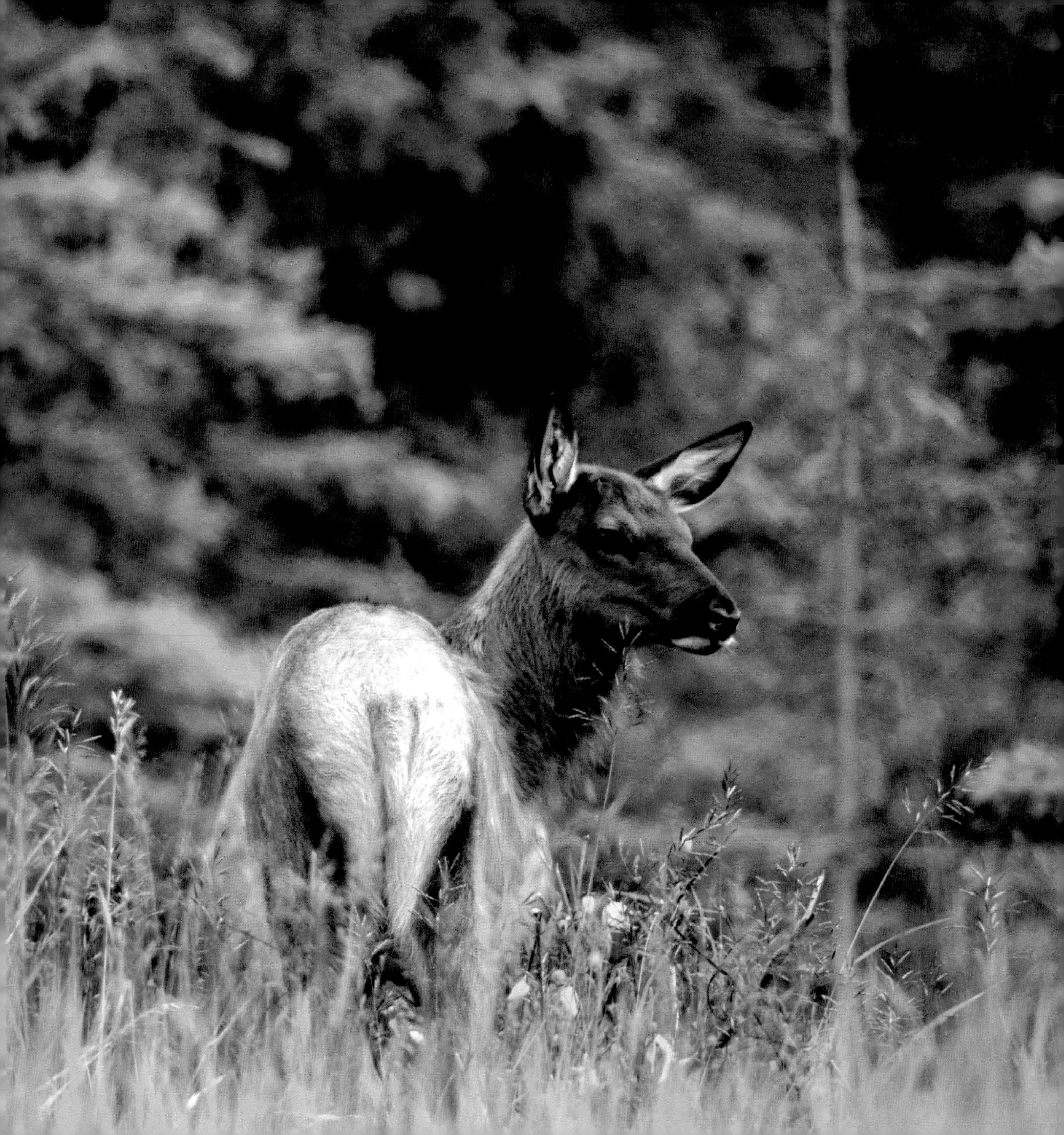

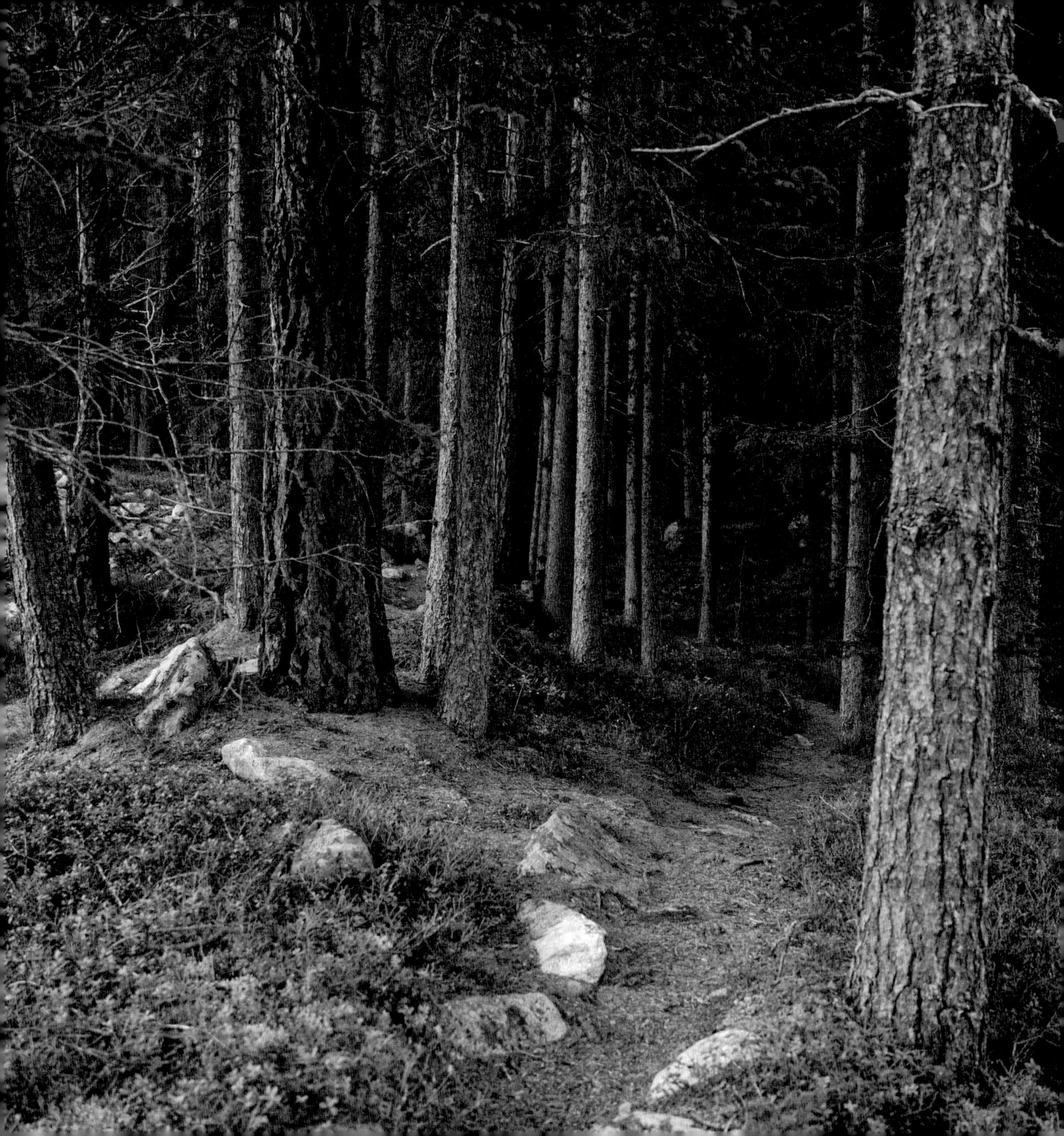

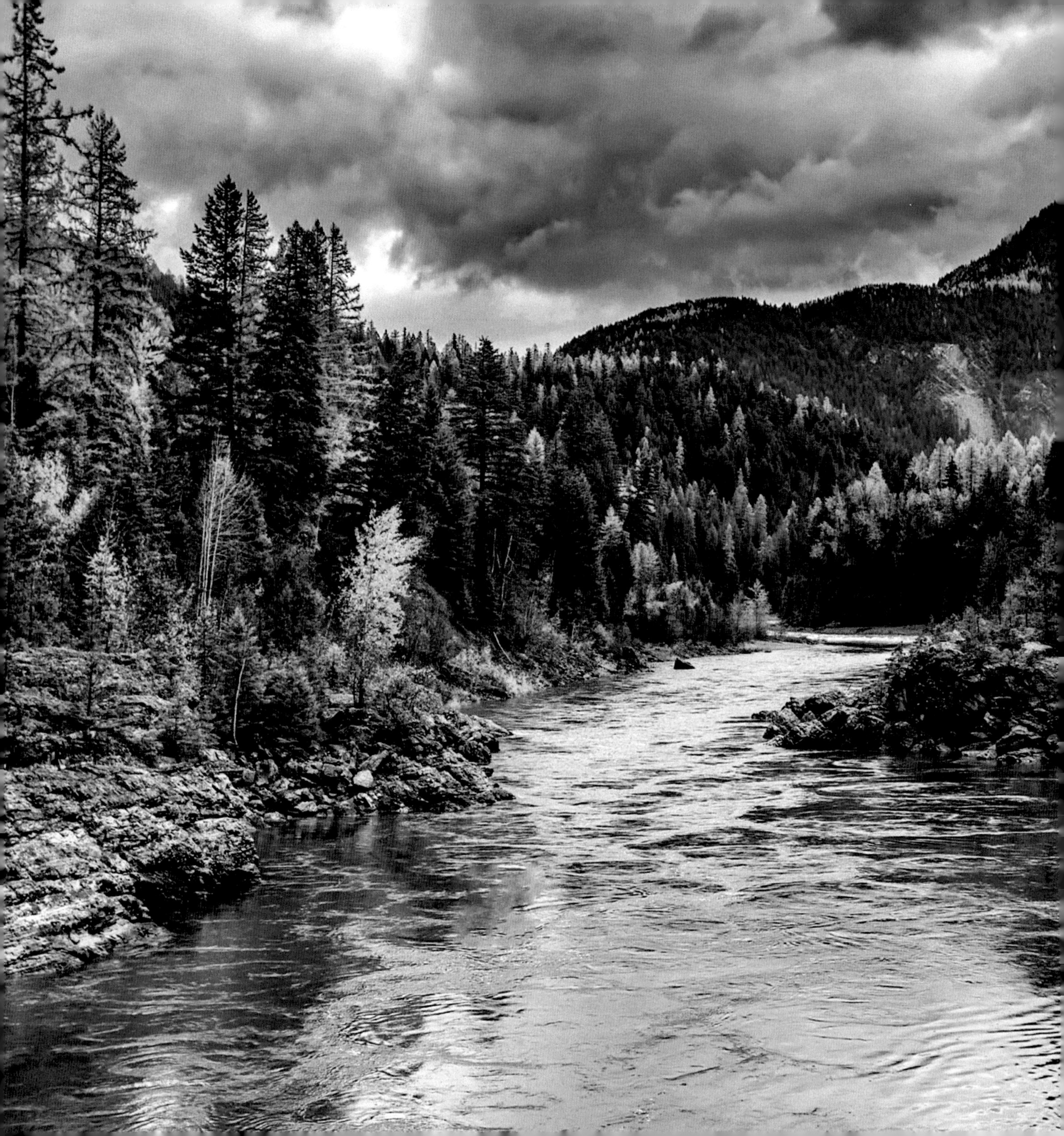

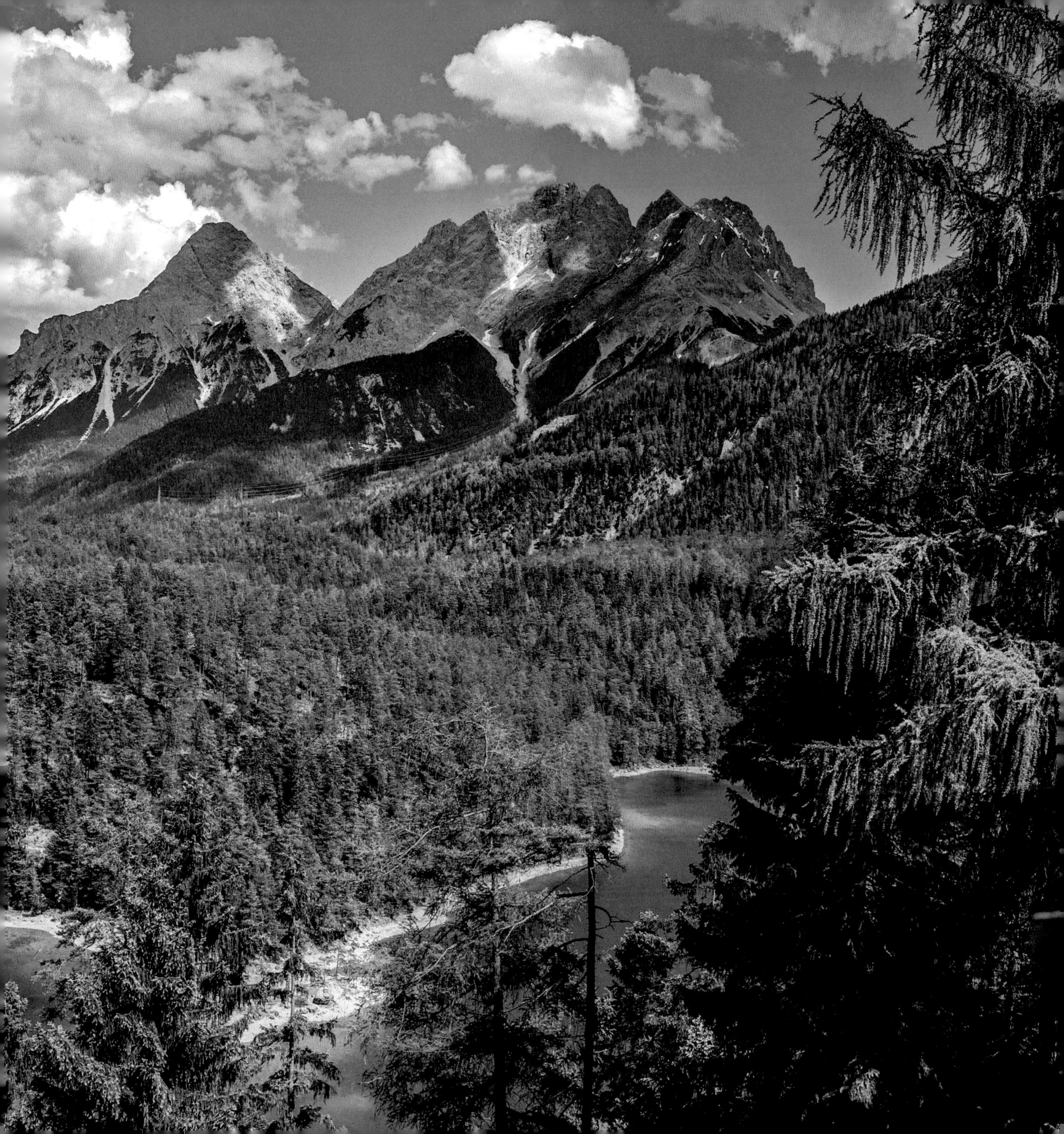

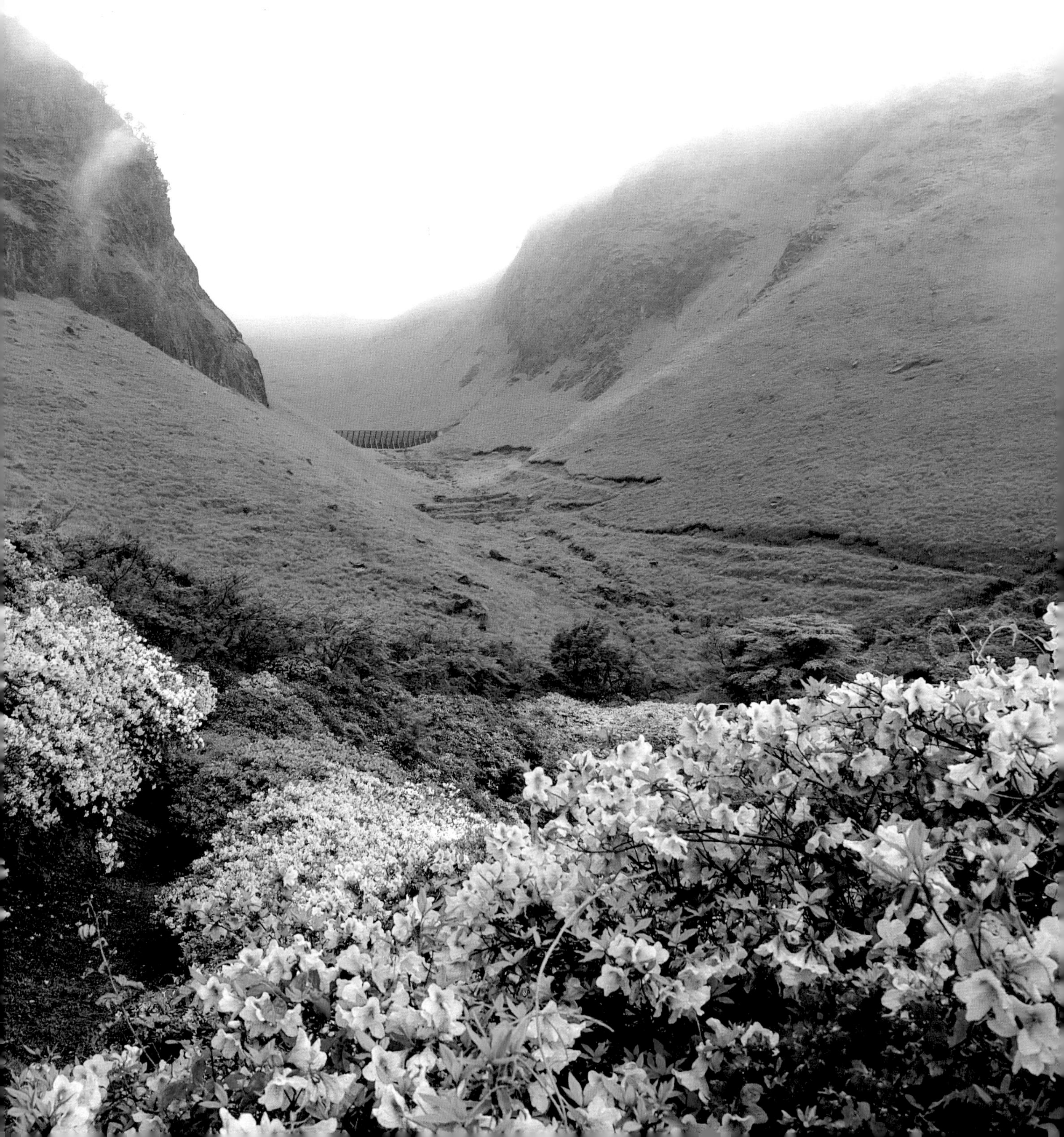

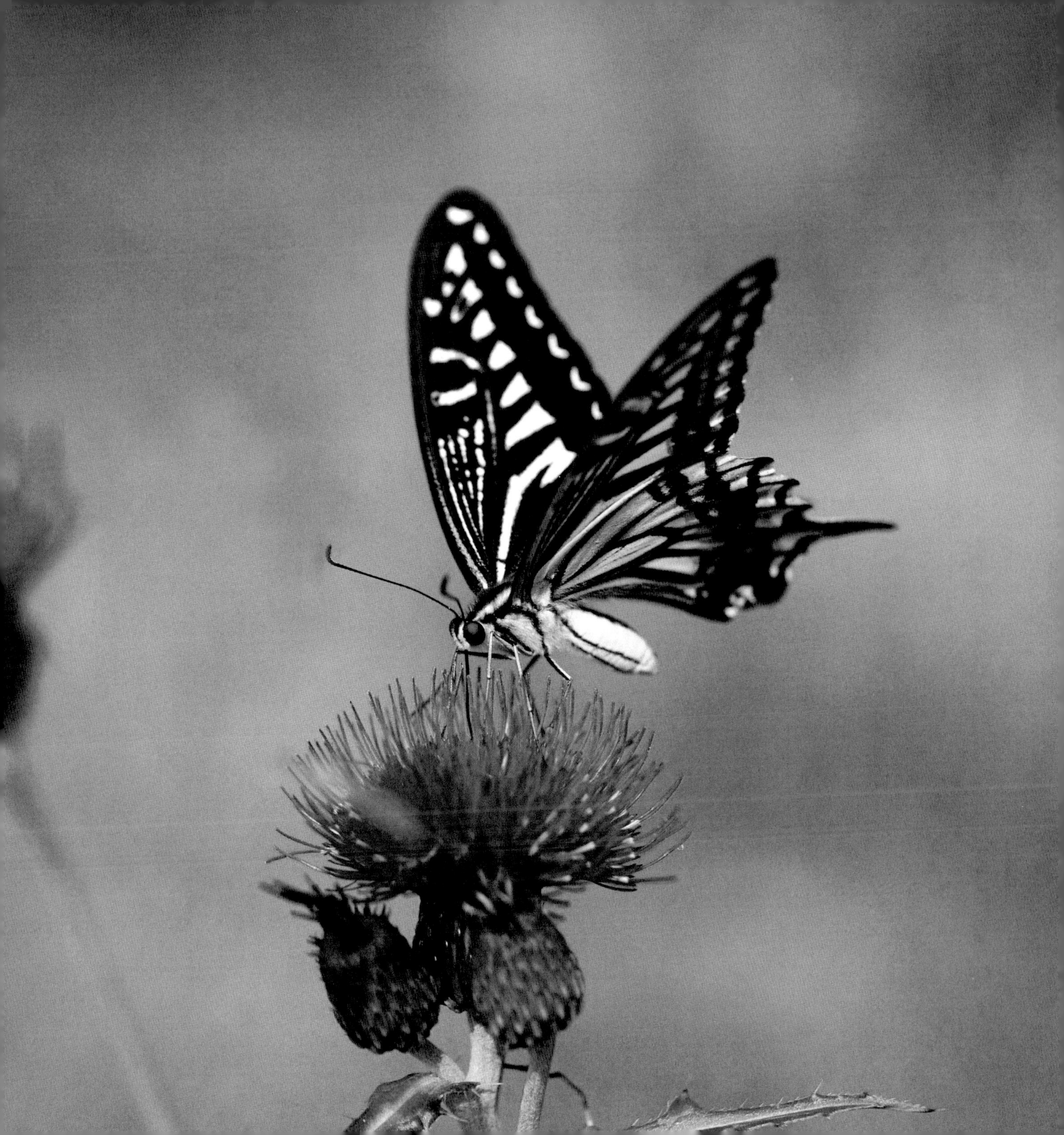

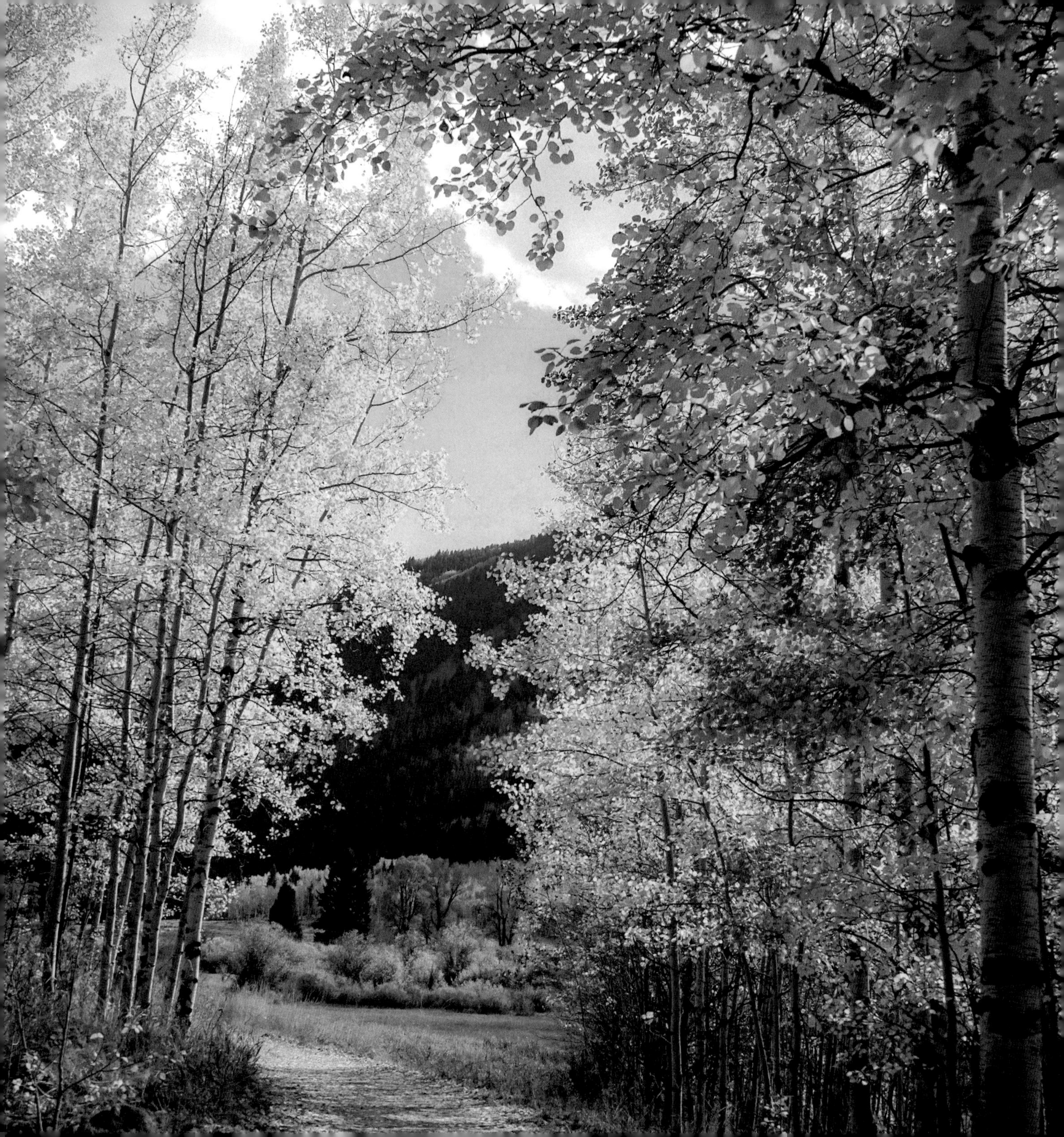

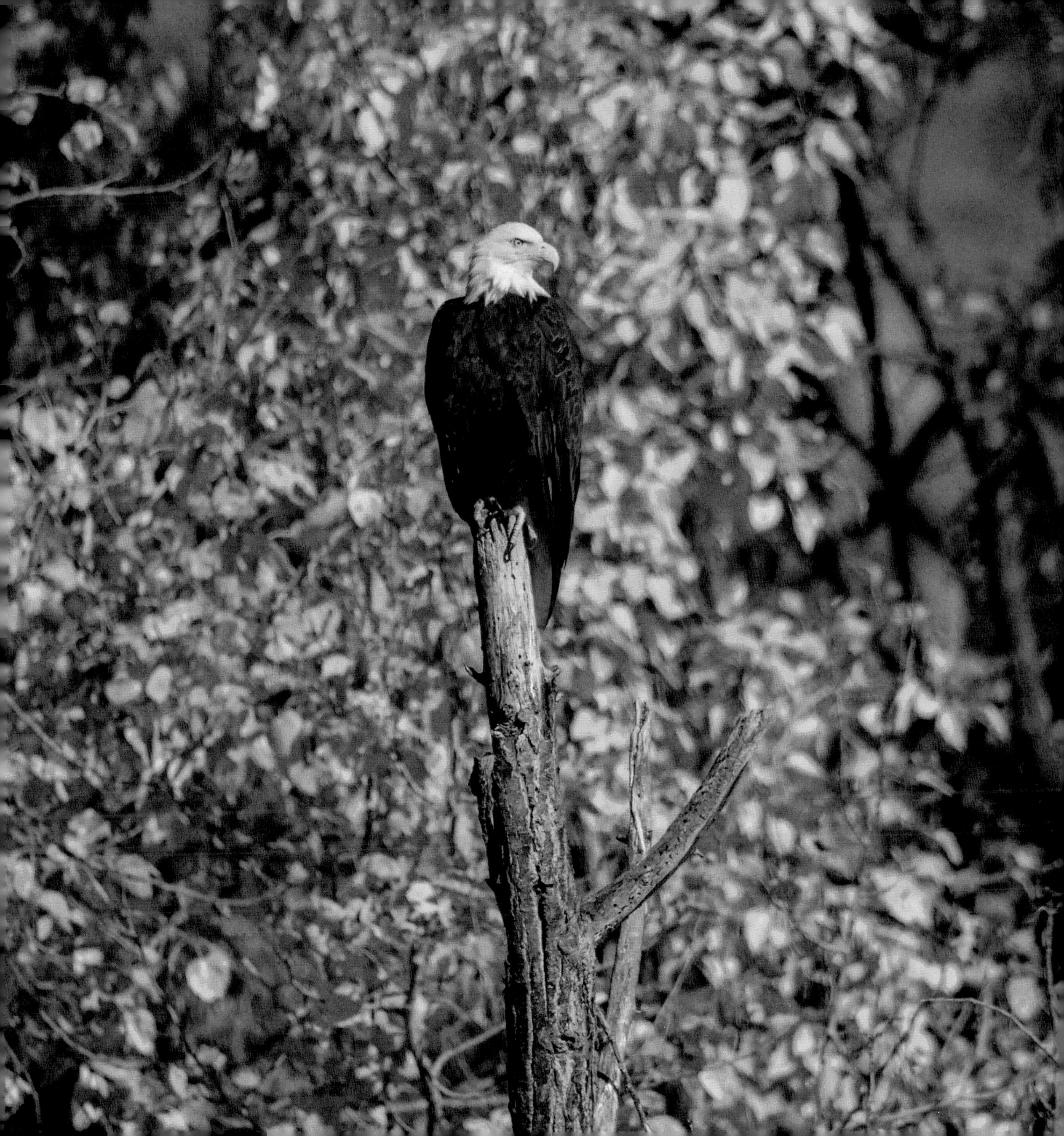

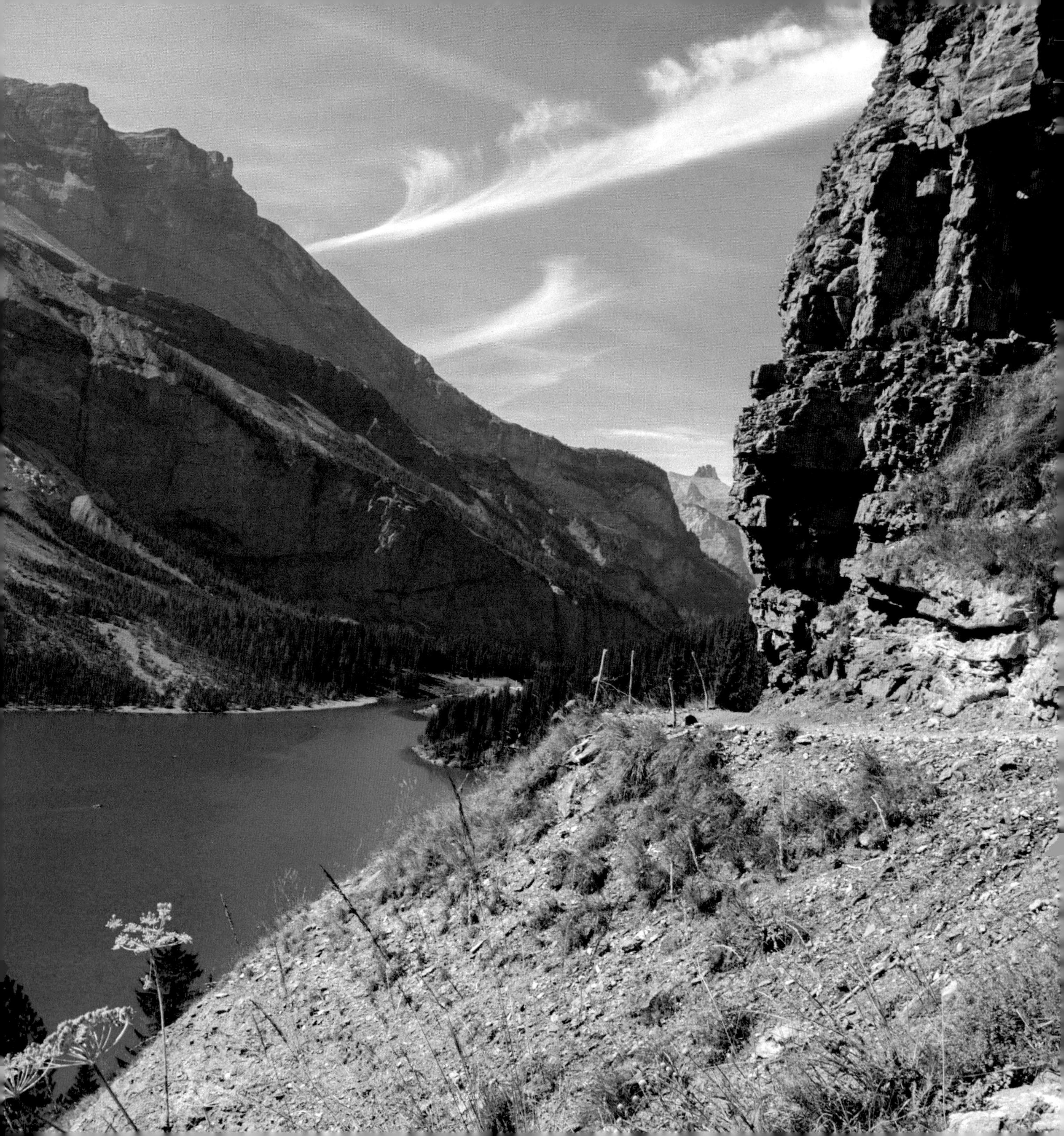

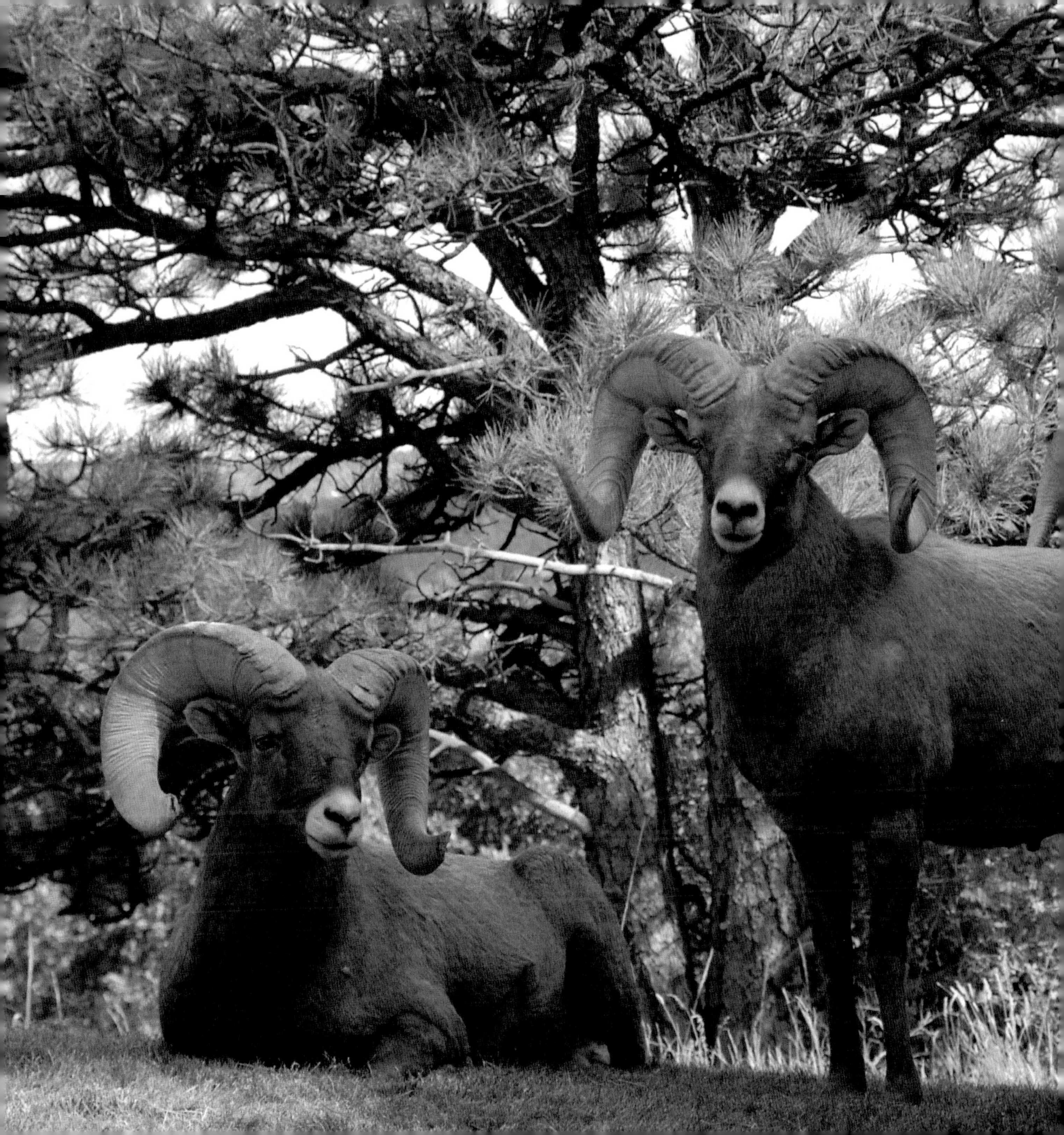

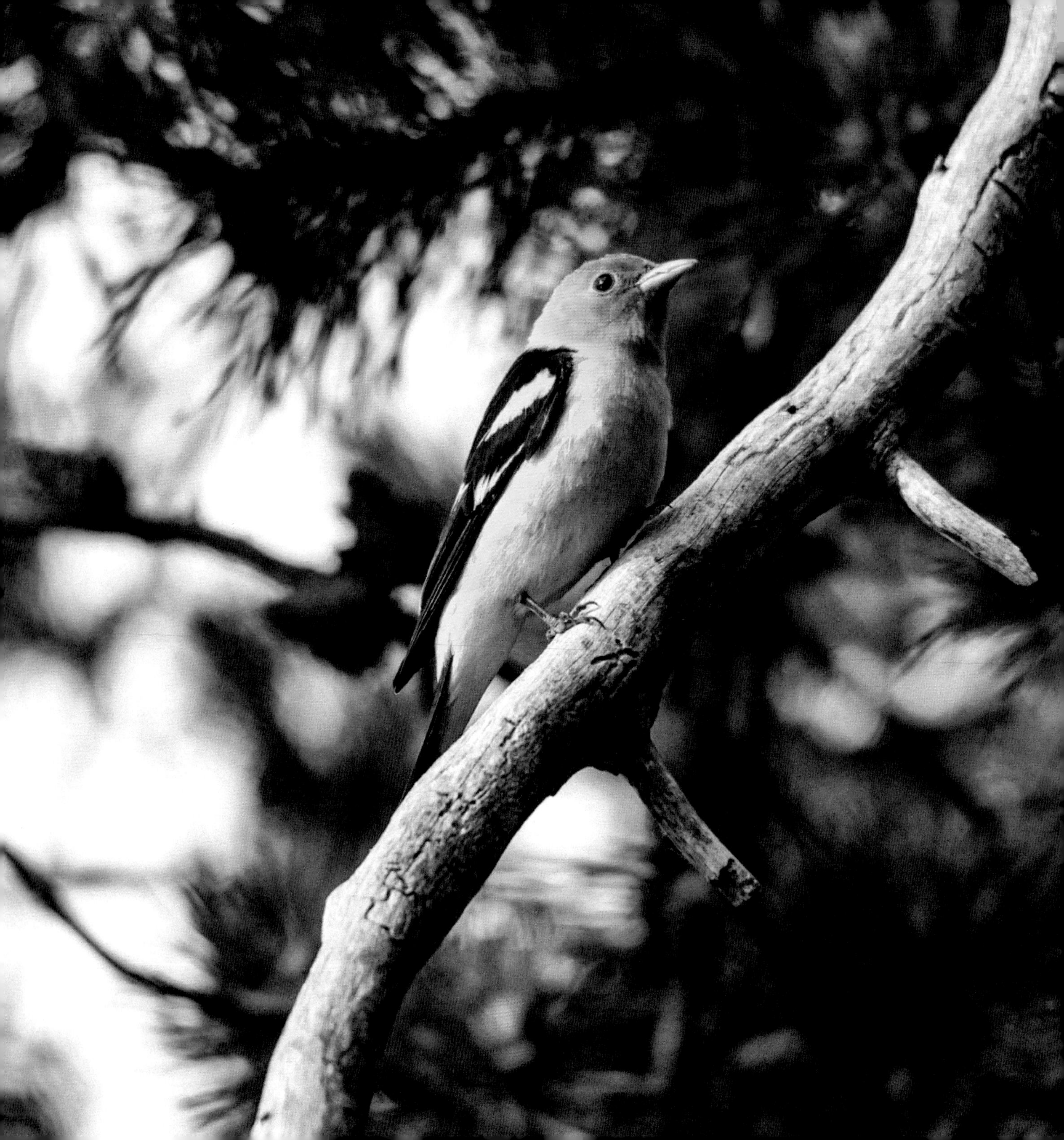

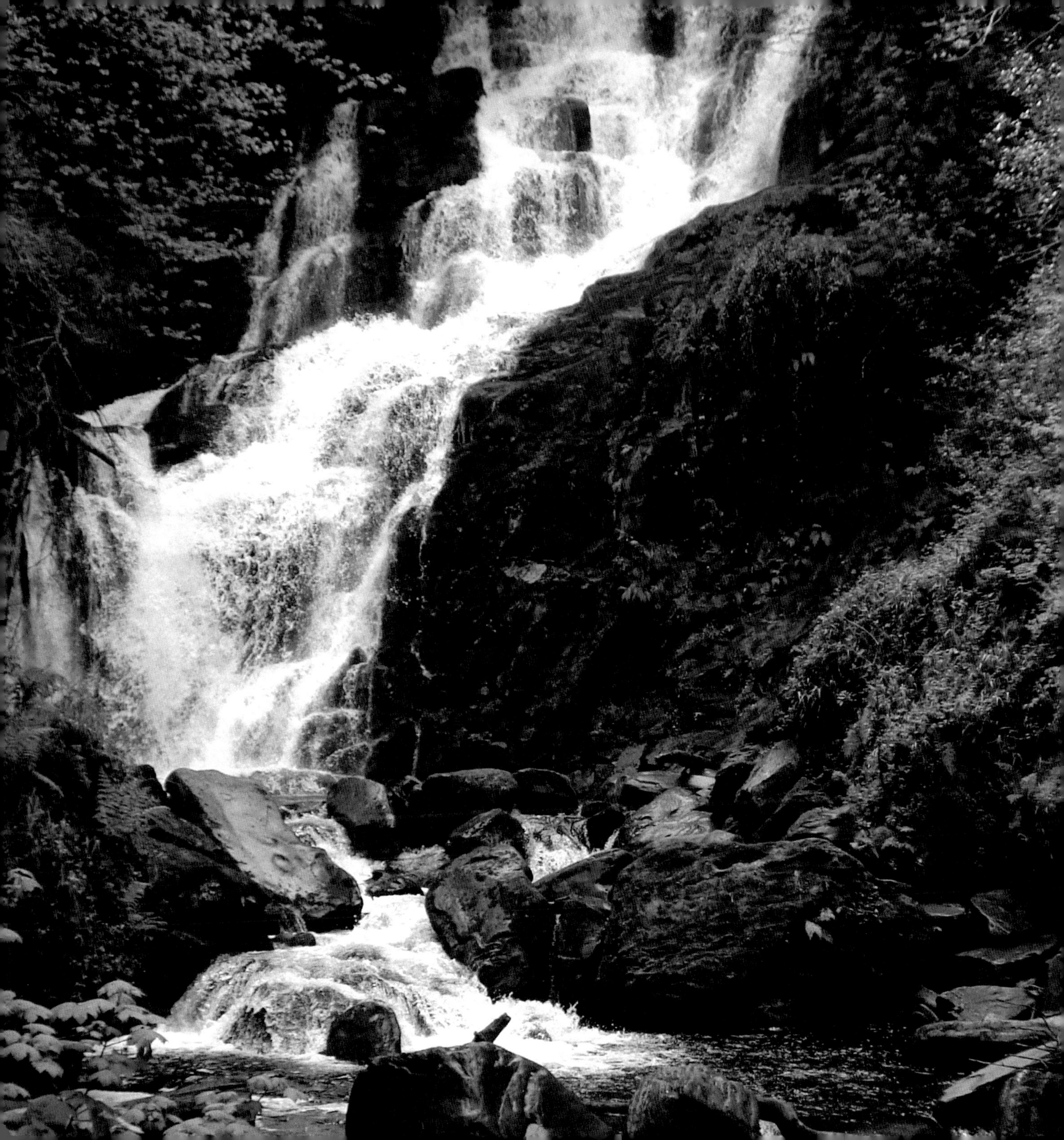

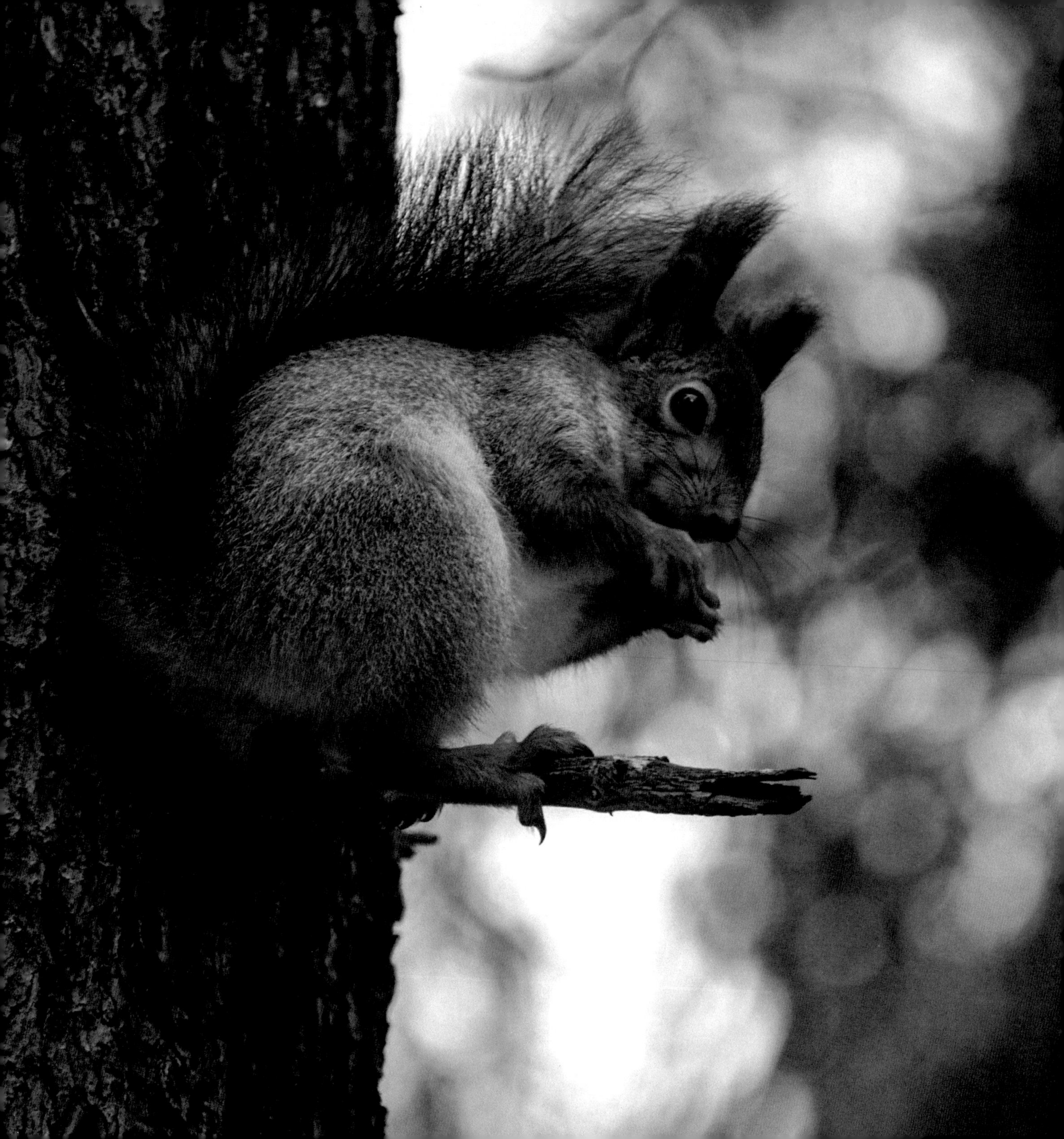

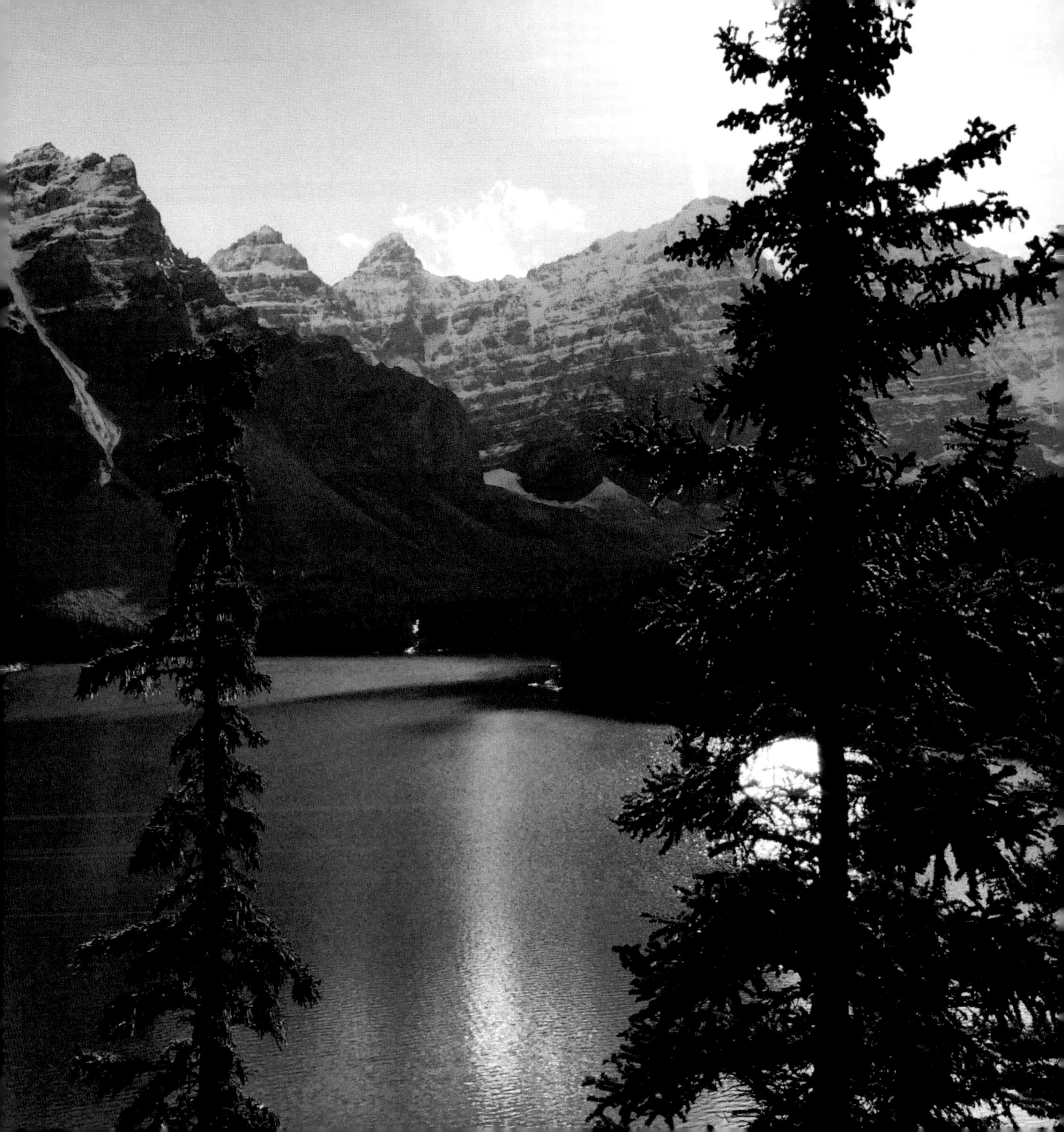

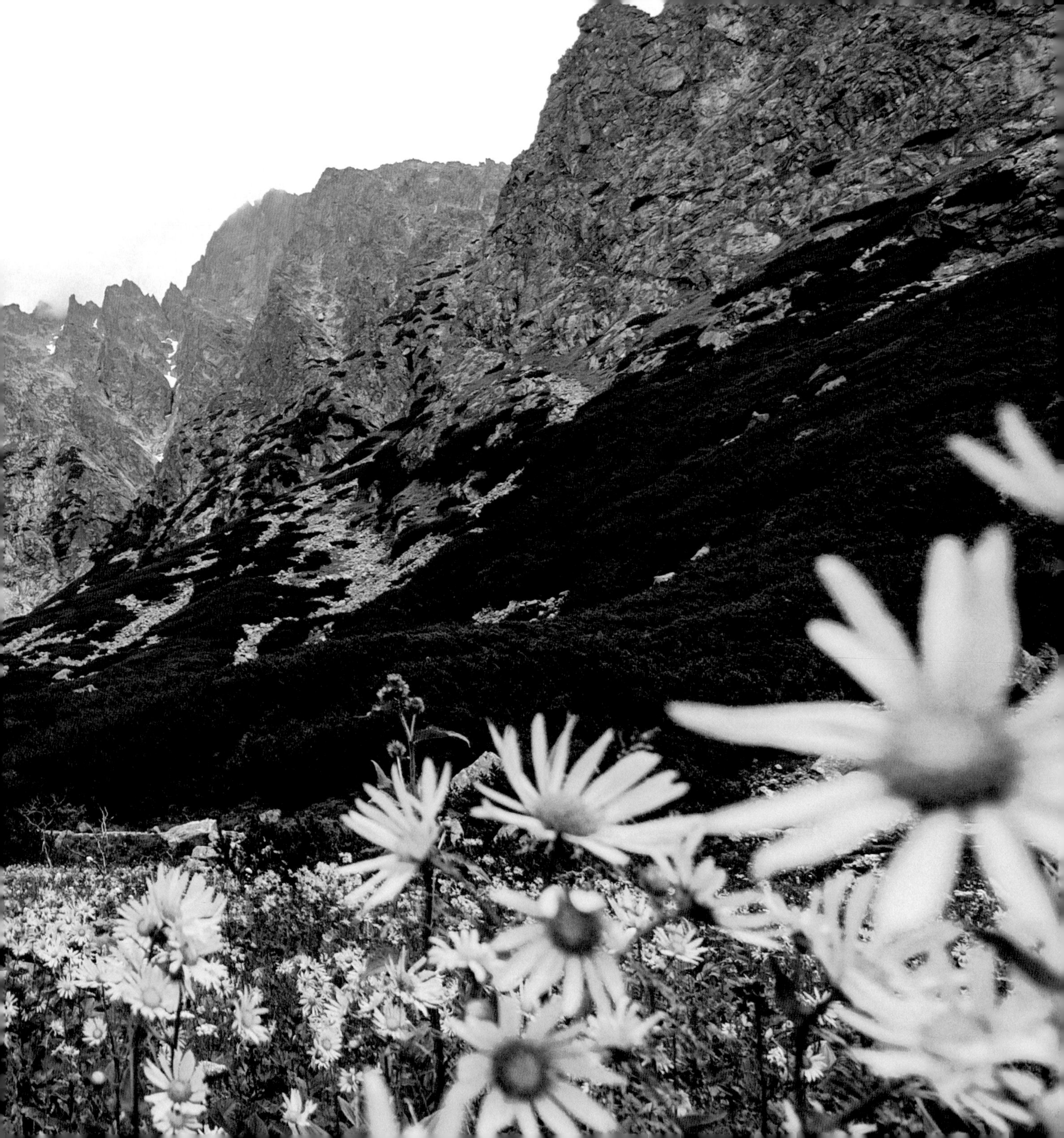

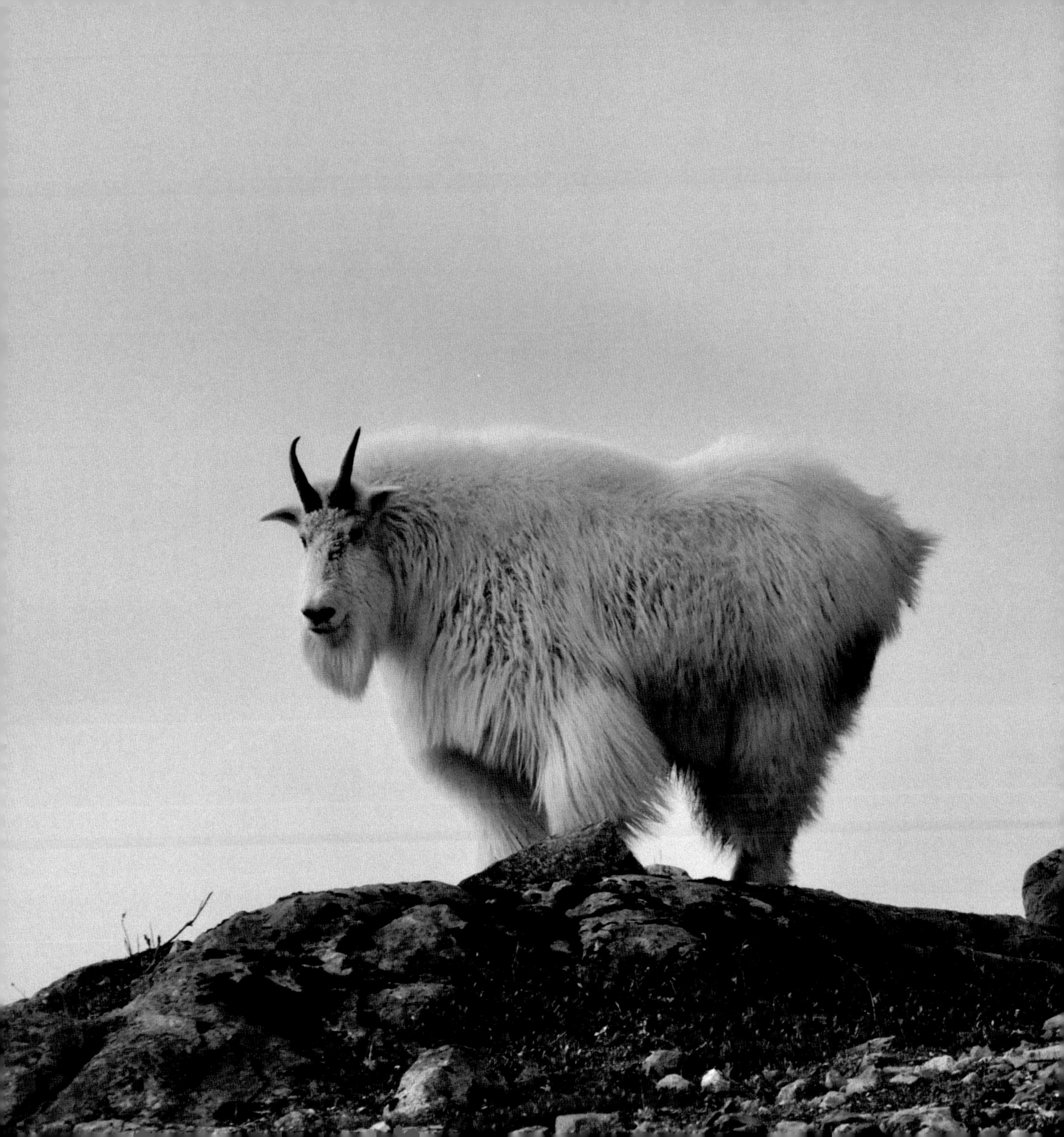

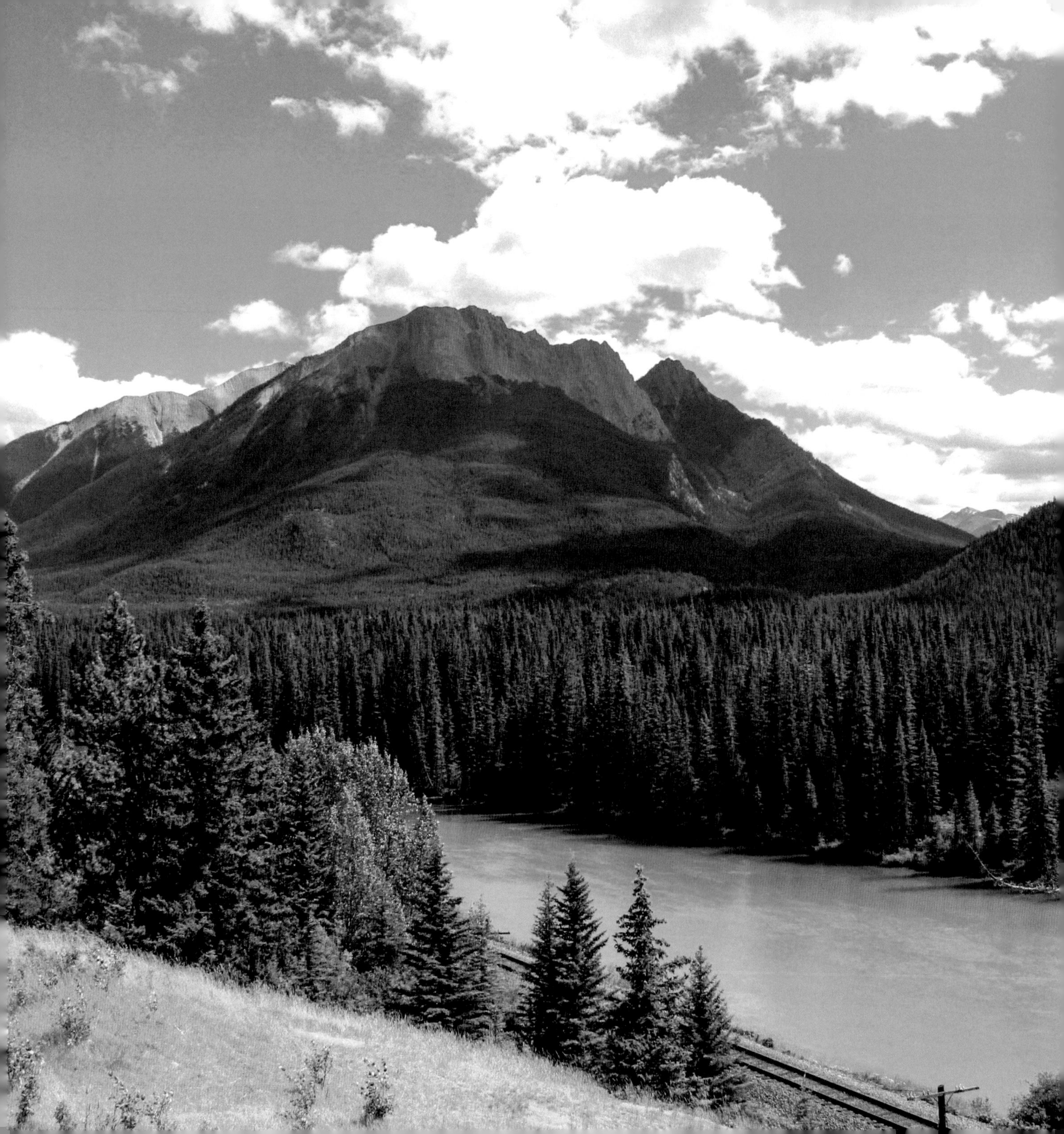

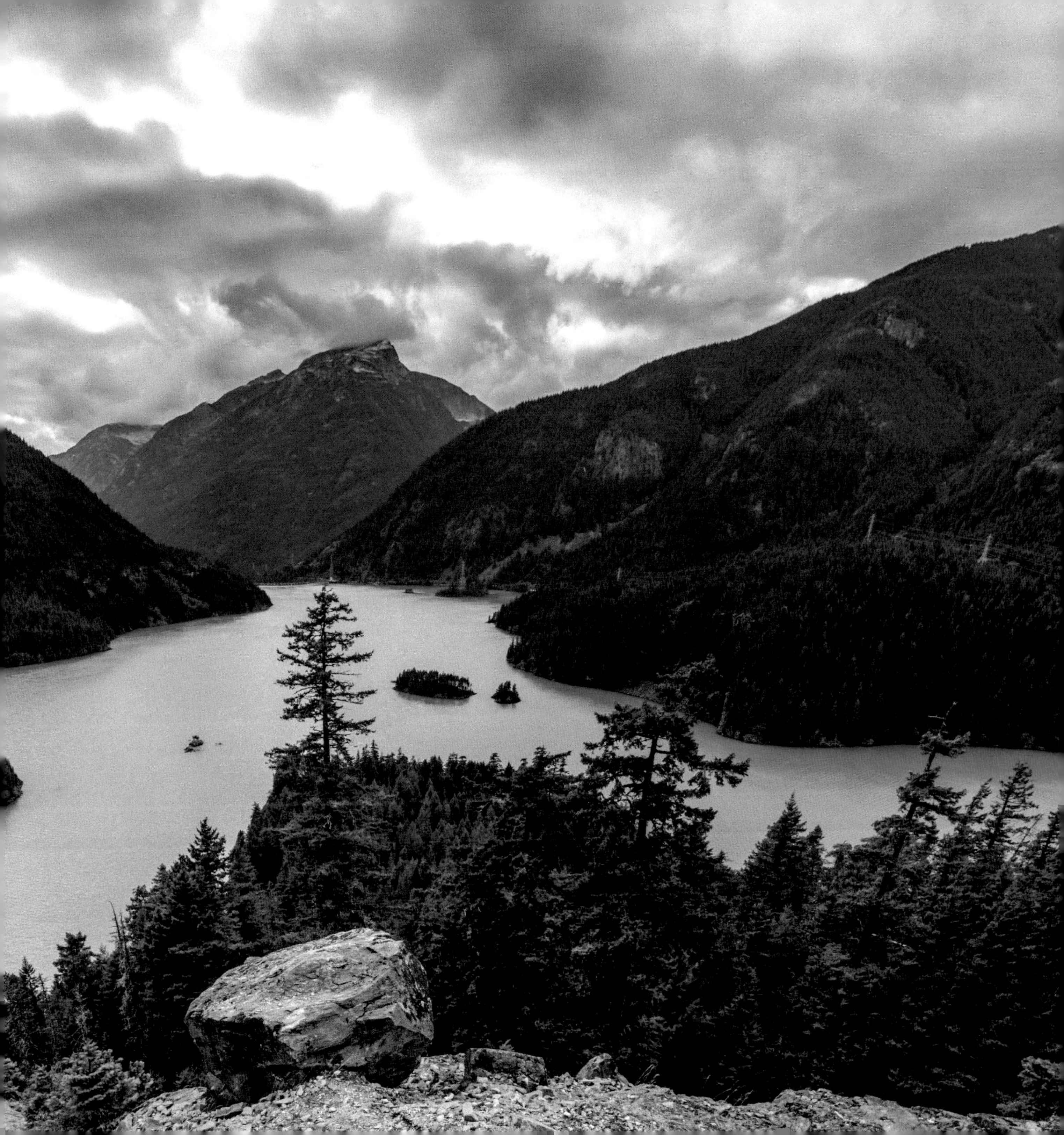

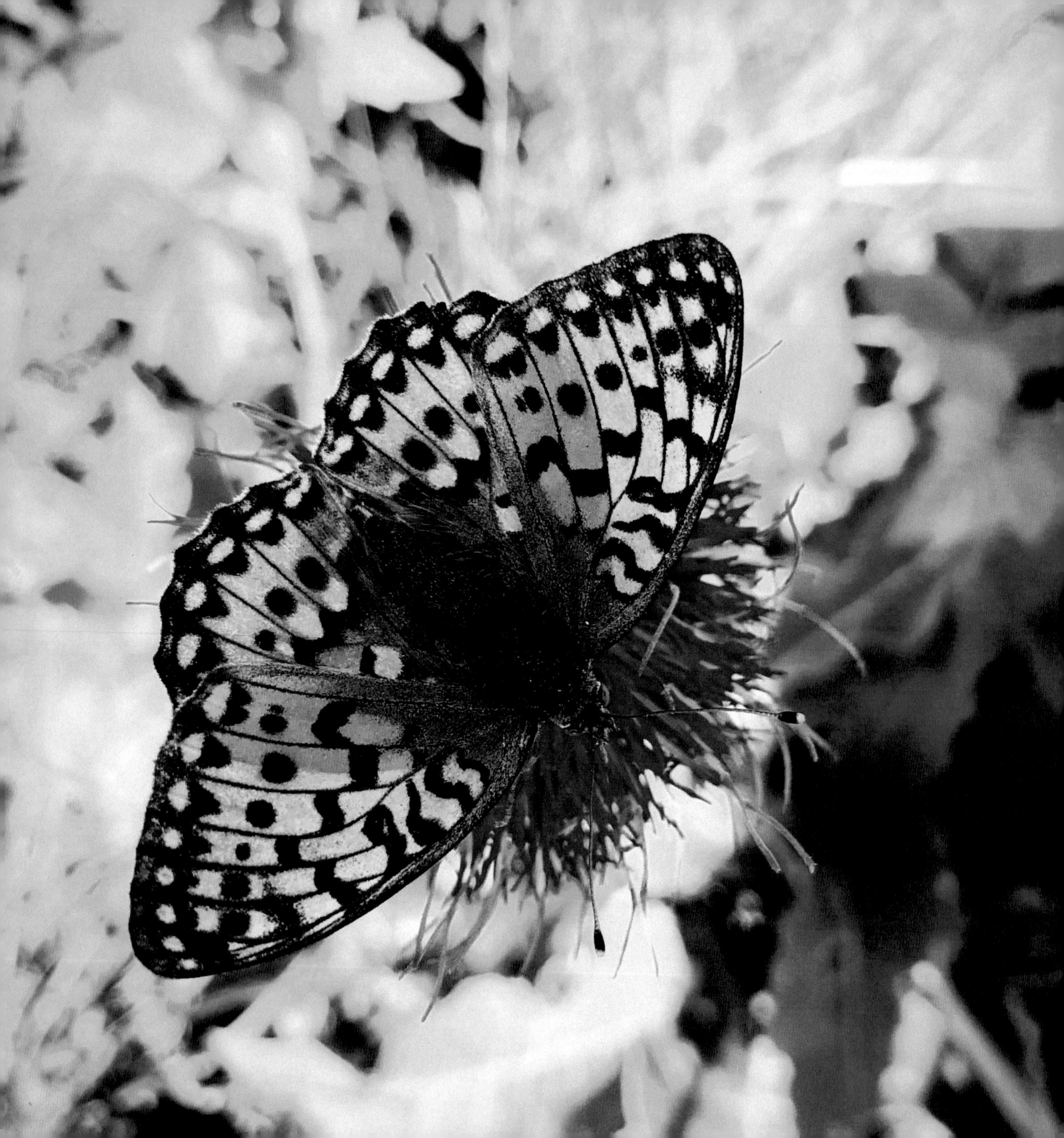

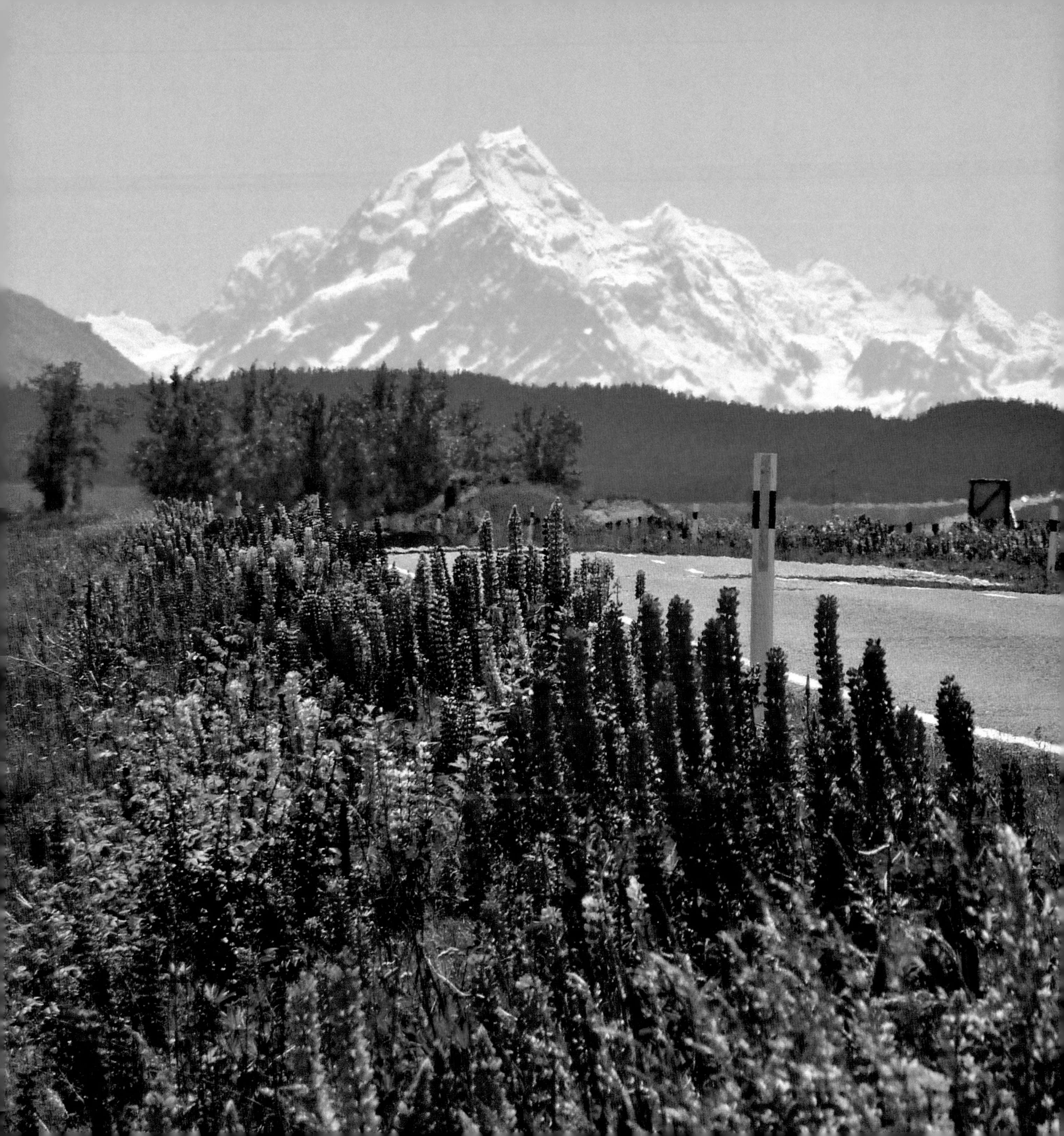

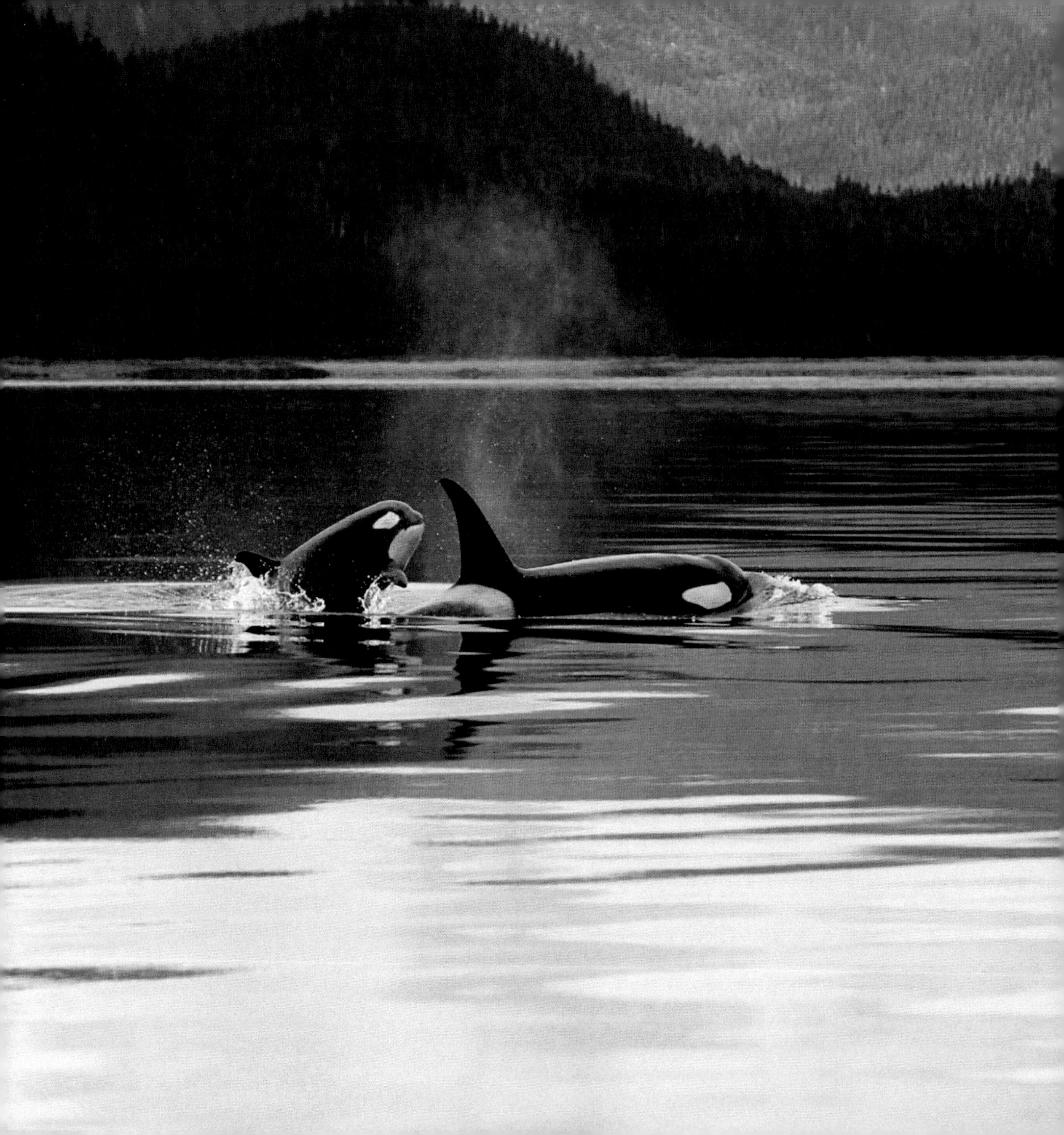

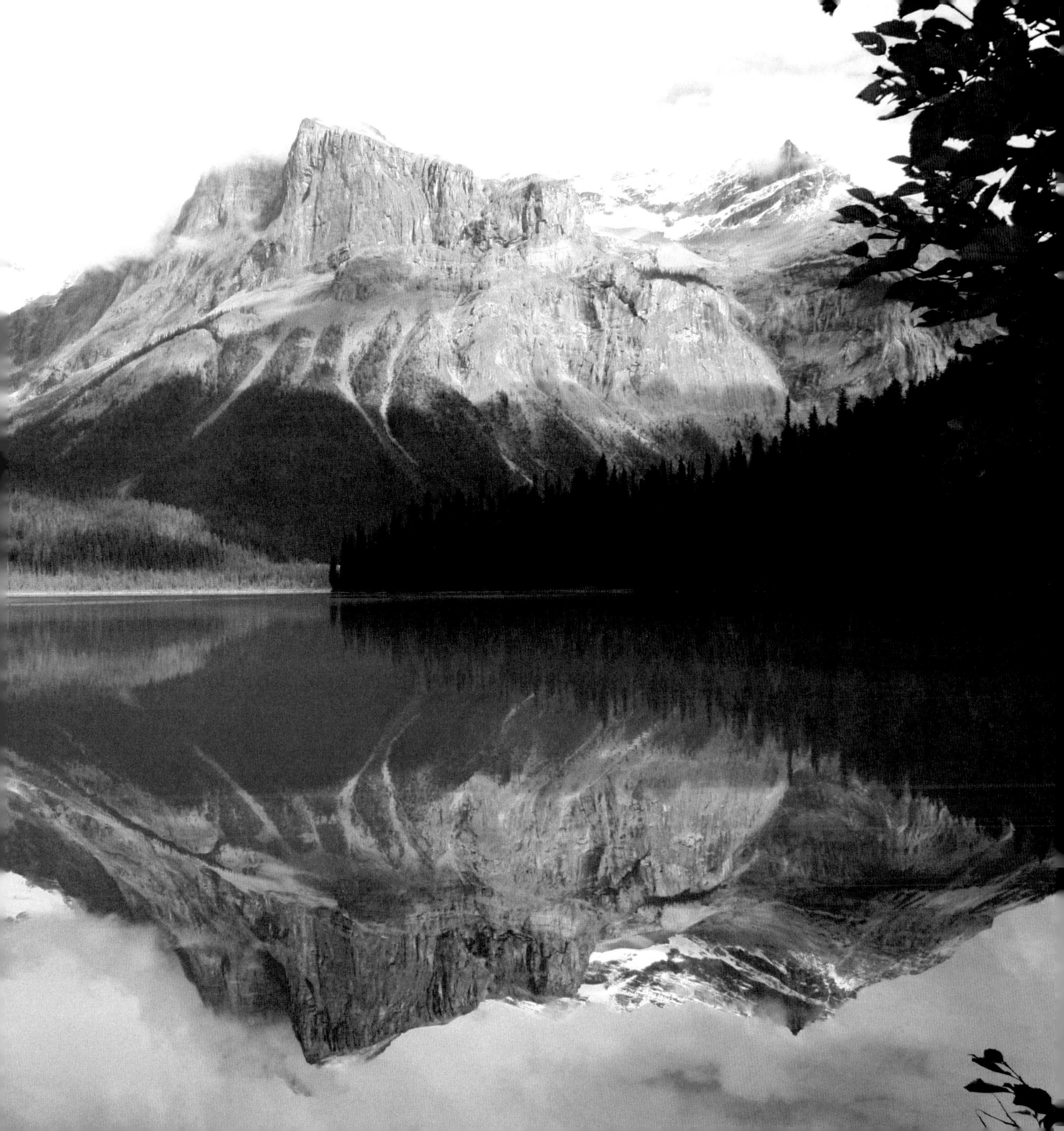

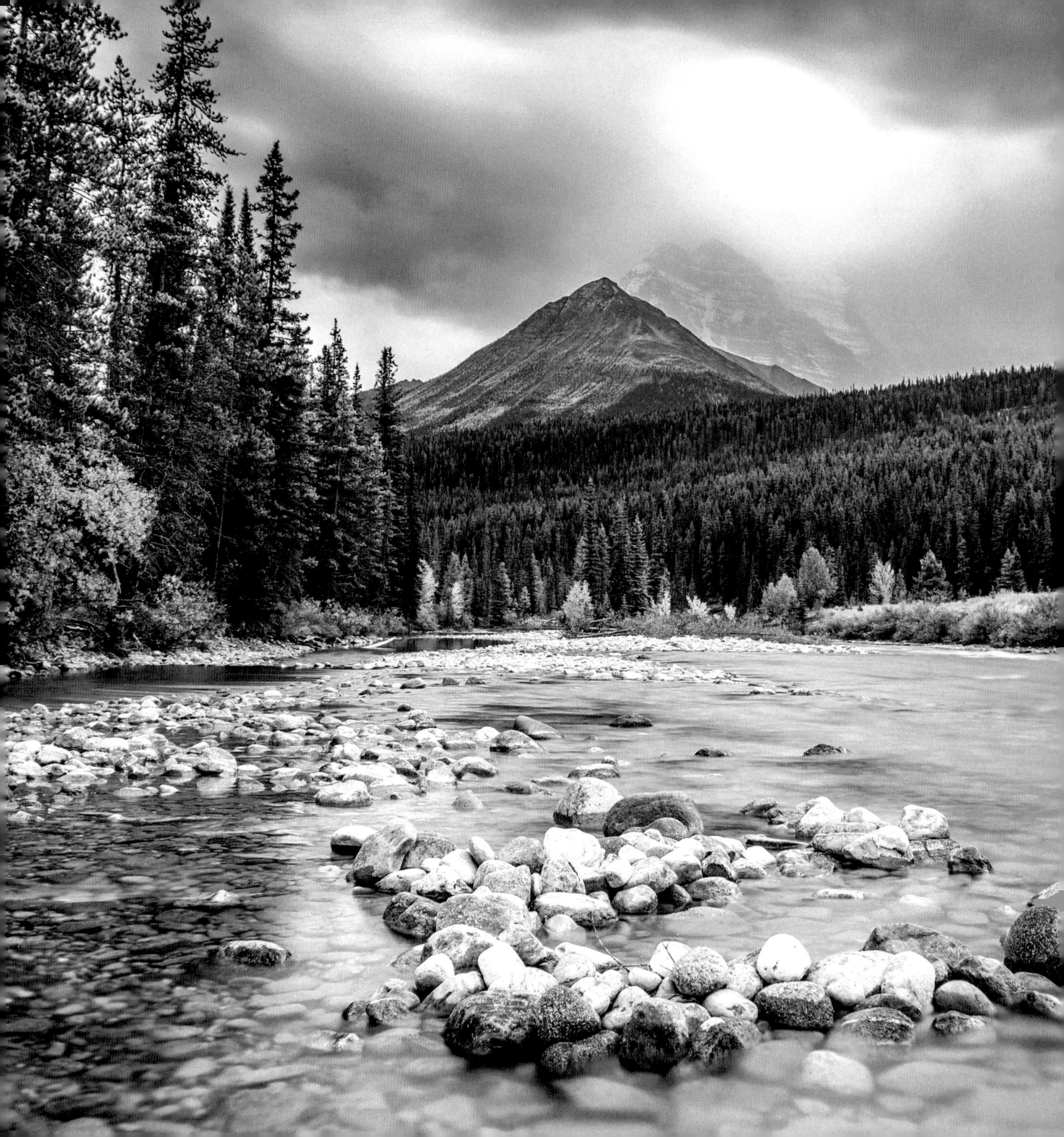

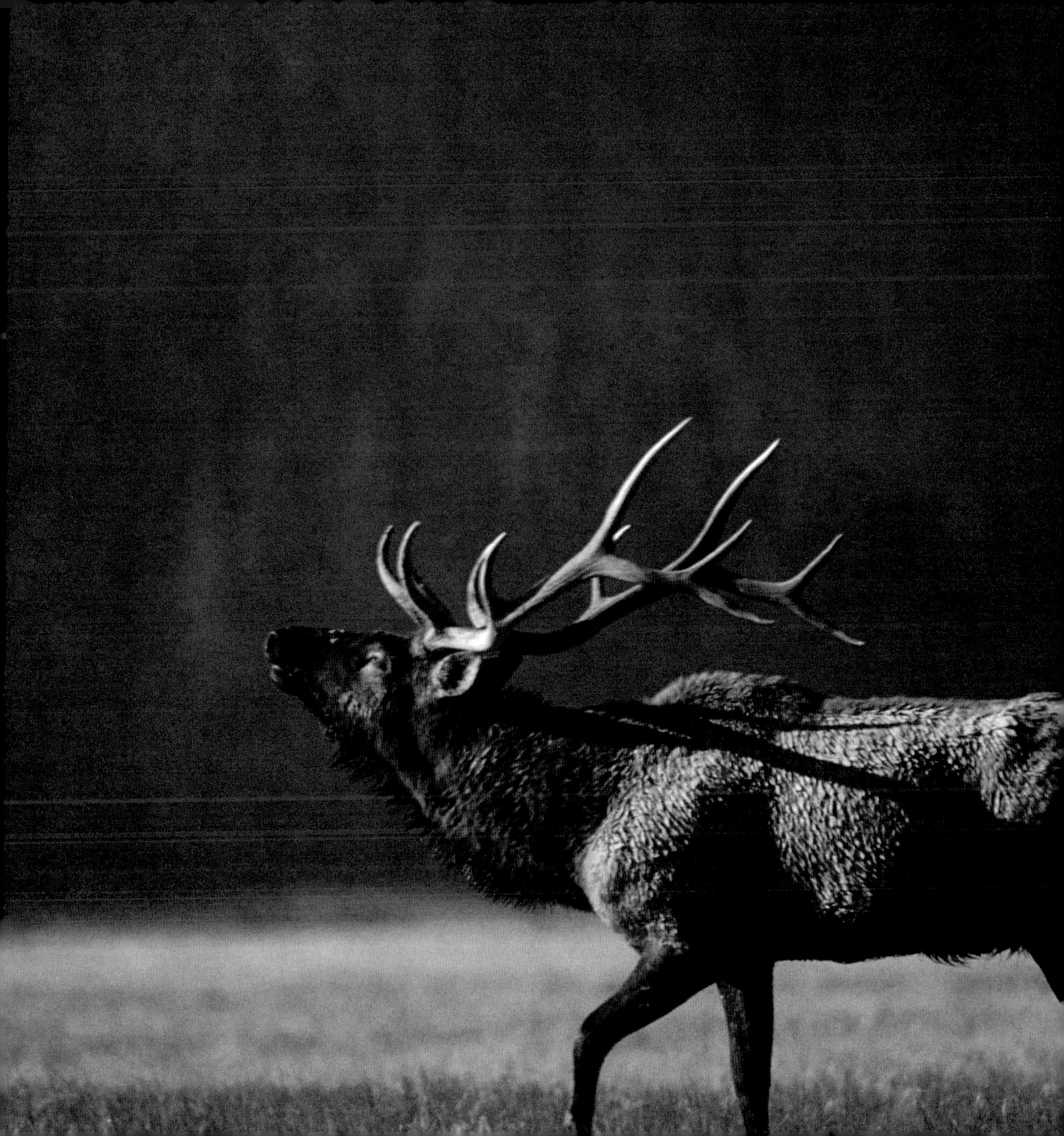

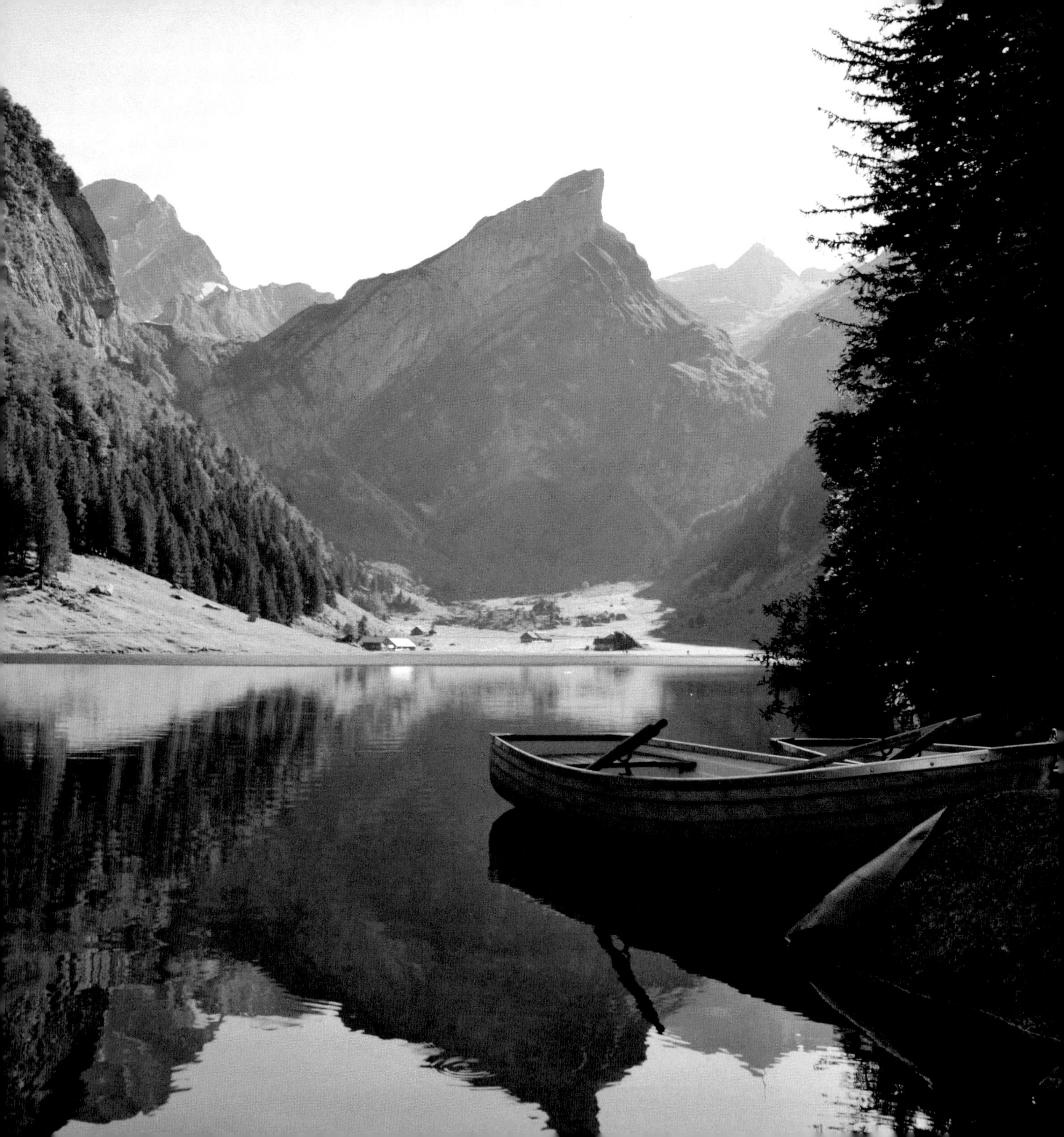

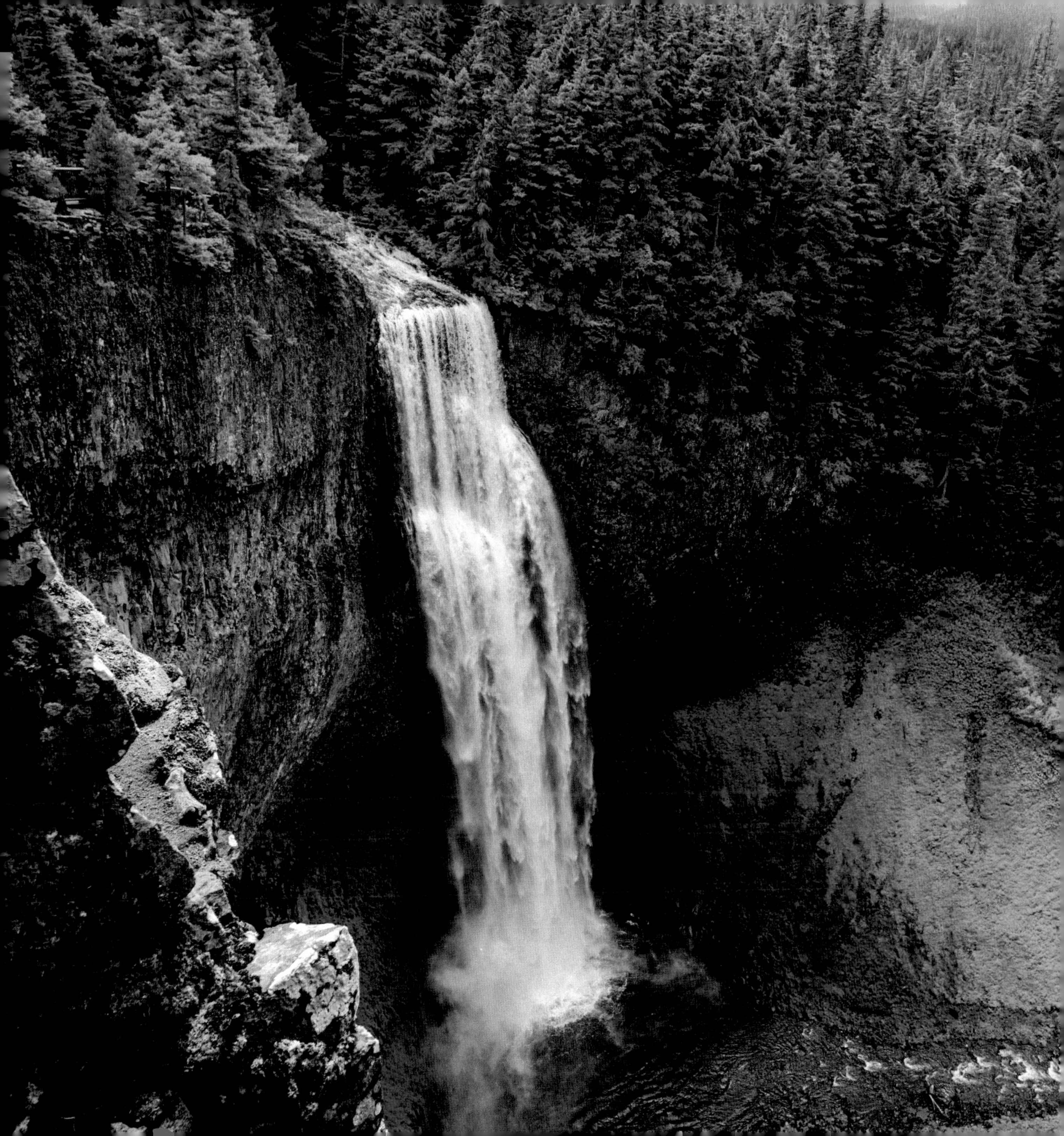

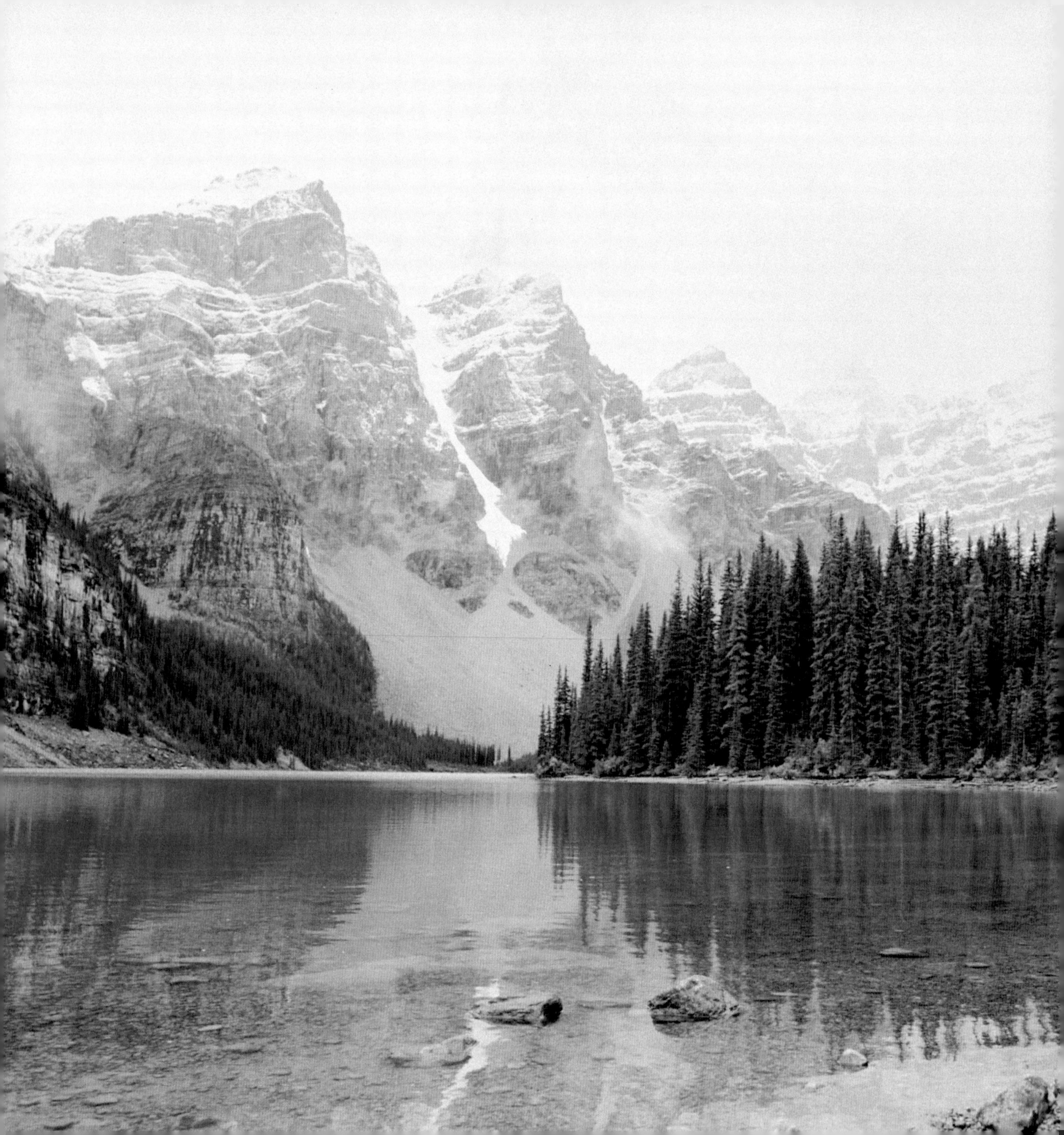

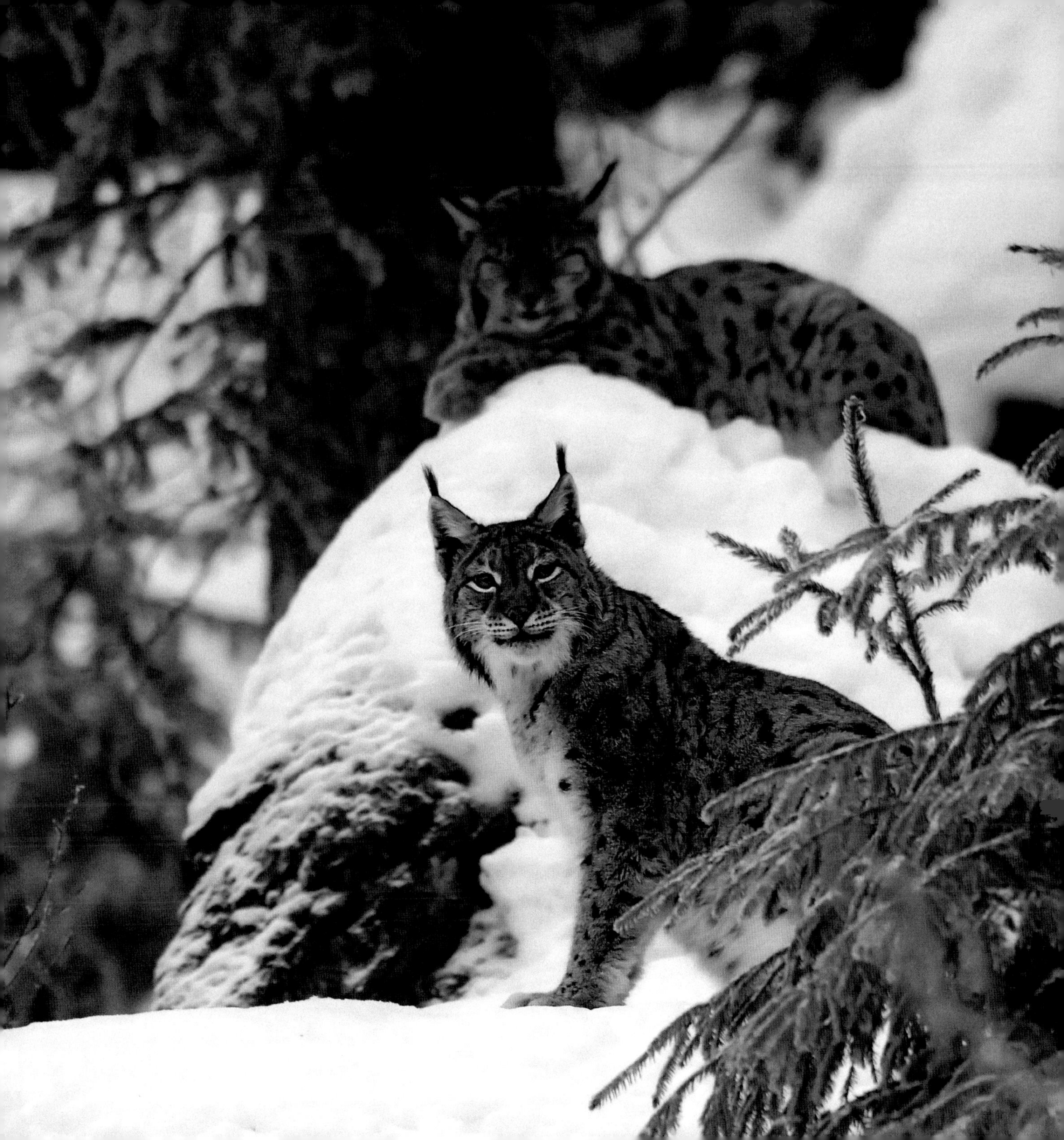

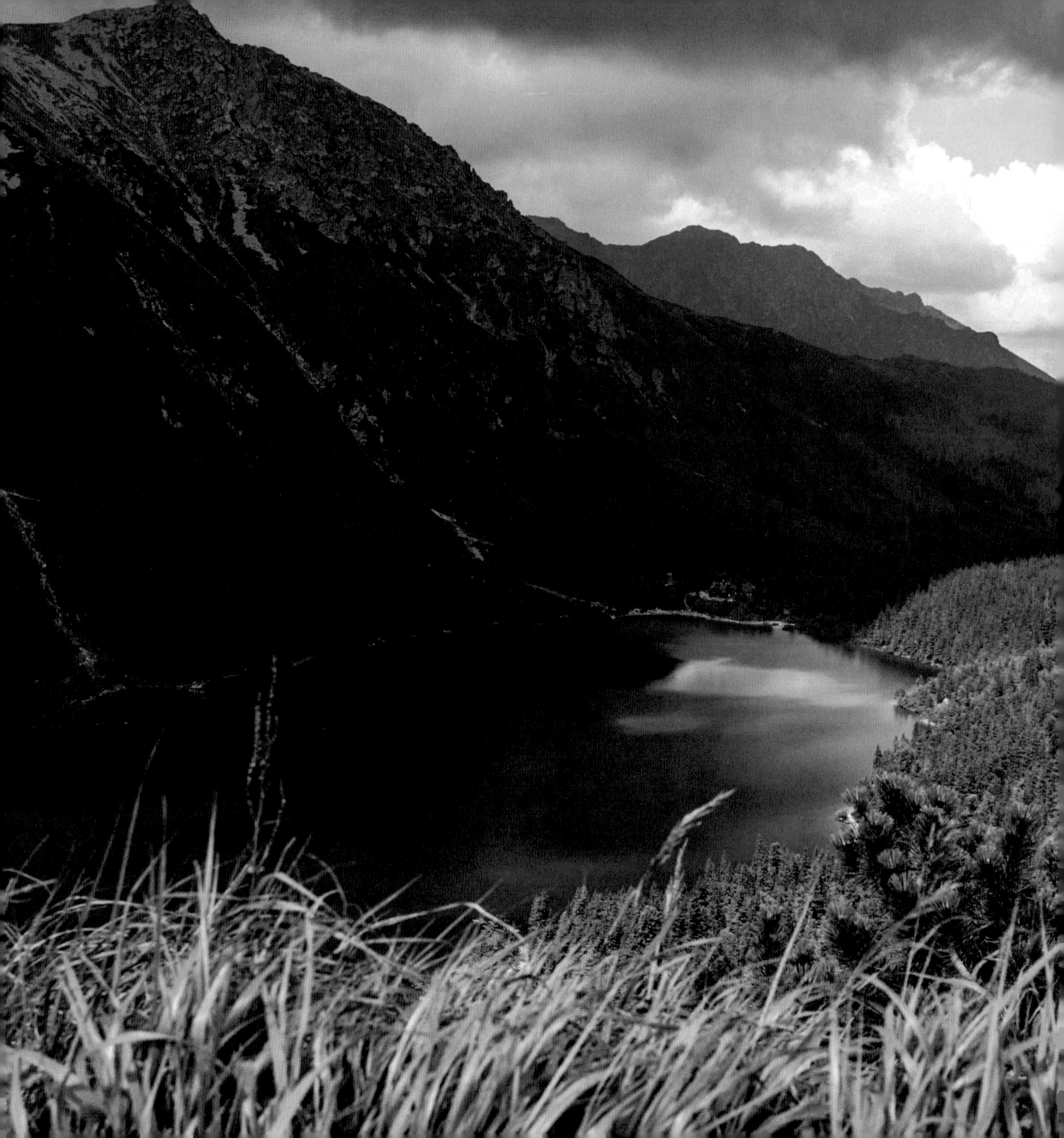

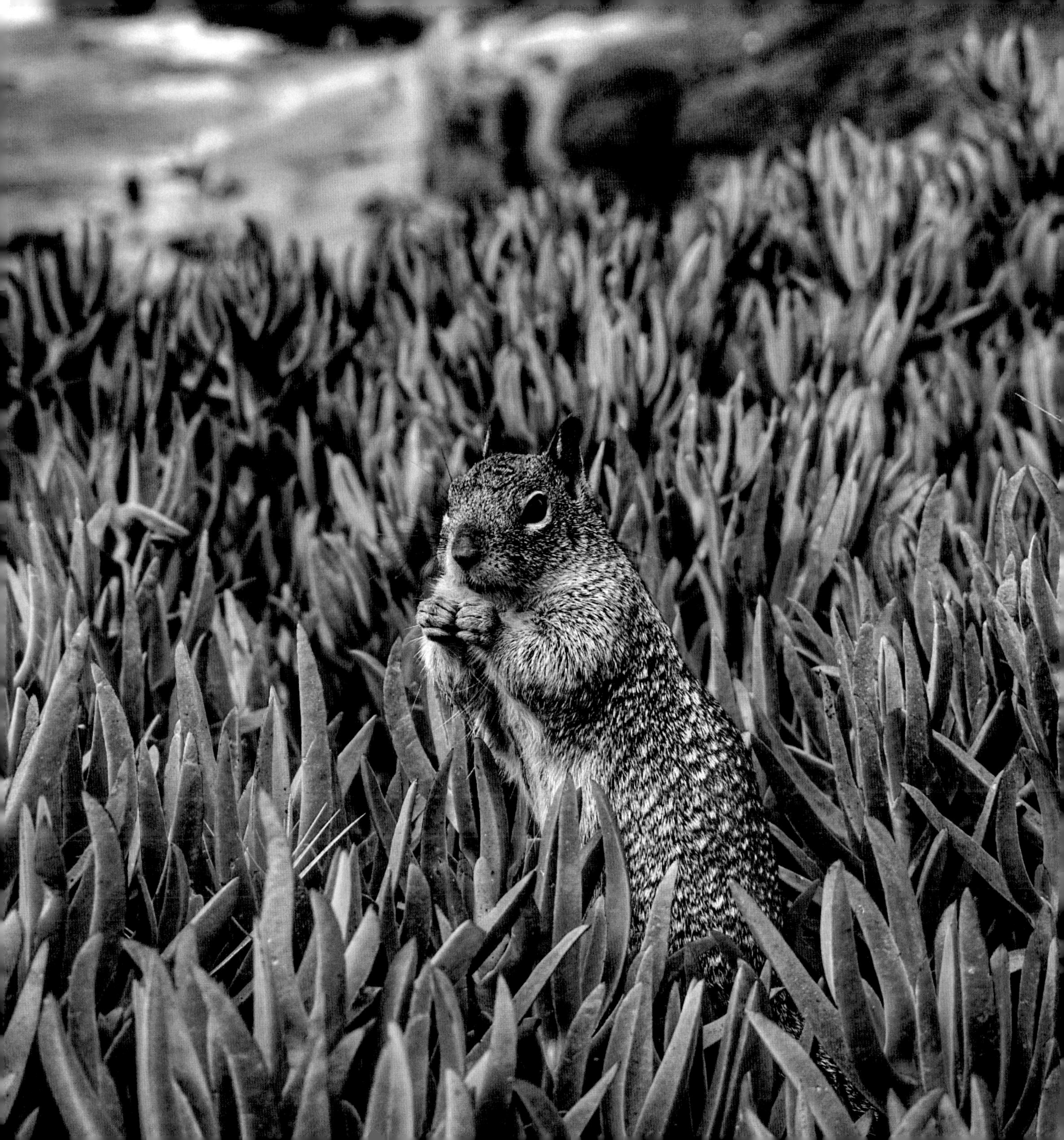

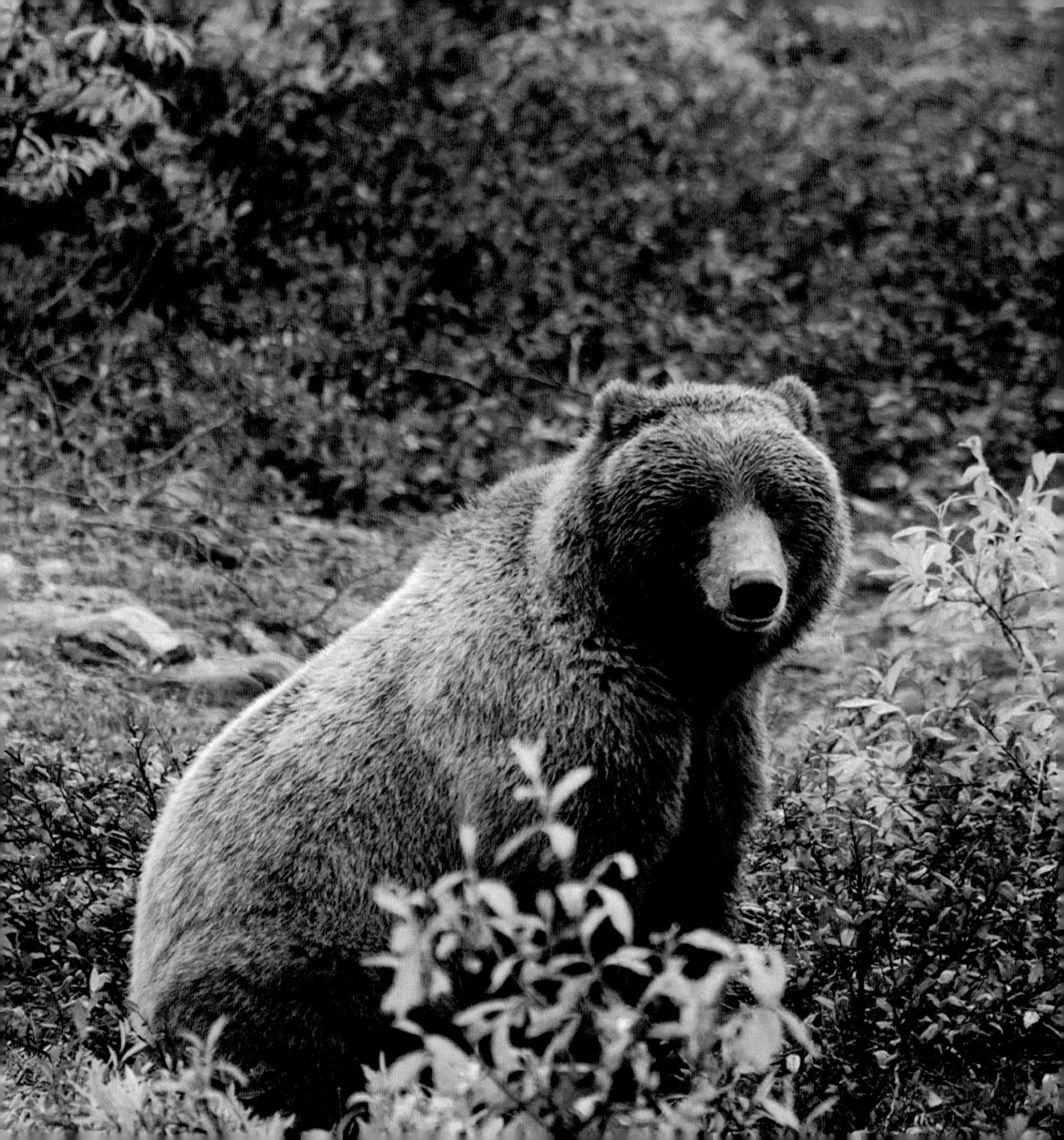

Made in the USA
Coppell, TX
26 December 2024

43548866R00026